Literacy Learning in Networked Classrooms

Using the Internet With Middle-Level Students

Mary L. McNabb

with Bonnie B. Thurber, Balazs Dibuz,
Pamela A. McDermott, and Carol Ann Lee

INTERNATIONAL
Reading Association
800 BARKSDALE ROAD, PO BOX 8139
NEWARK, DE 19714-8139, USA
www.reading.org

The International Reading Association attempts, through its publications, to provide a forum for a wide spectrum of opinions on reading. This policy permits divergent viewpoints without implying the endorsement of the Association.

Director of Publications Dan Mangan
Editorial Director, Books and Special Projects Teresa Curto
Managing Editor, Books Shannon T. Fortner
Acquisitions and Developmental Editor Corinne M. Mooney
Associate Editor Charlene M. Nichols
Associate Editor Elizabeth C. Hunt
Production Editor Amy Messick
Books and Inventory Assistant Rebecca A. Zell
Permissions Editor Janet S. Parrack
Assistant Permissions Editor Tyanna L. Collins
Production Department Manager Iona Muscella
Supervisor, Electronic Publishing Anette Schütz
Senior Electronic Publishing Specialist R. Lynn Harrison
Electronic Publishing Specialist Lisa M. Kochel
Proofreader Stacey Lynn Sharp

Project Editor Elizabeth C. Hunt

Cover Design, Linda Steere; Illustration, ImageZoo/Images.com

Web addresses in this book were correct as of the publication date but may have become inactive or otherwise modified since that time. If you notice a deactivated or changed Web address, please e-mail books@reading.org with the words "Website Update" in the subject line. In your message, specify the Web link, the book title, and the page number on which the link appears.

Library of Congress Cataloging-in-Publication Data
McNabb, Mary L.
  Literacy learning in networked classrooms : using the Internet with middle-level students / Mary L. McNabb ; with Bonnie B. Thurber ... [et al.]
    p. cm.
  Includes bibliographical references and index.
  ISBN 0-87207-567-2
  1. Language arts (Secondary)--Computer-assisted instruction. 2. Computers and literacy. 3. Internet in education. 4. Virtual reality in education. I. Title: Using the Internet with middle-level students. II. Thurber, Bonnie B. III. Title.
  LB1631.M32 2005
  428.0071'2--dc22
                                                                              2005031636

Dedicated to my parents, Janet and Cal,
who taught me the value of literacy.

CONTENTS

My awareness of technology's impact on literacy first began in the early 1980s when I learned word processing. The simple act of backspacing to delete letters I had typed on the computer screen was at once astounding and intriguing. Cut and paste functions were equally amazing. My fascination with computers grew when, in the 1990s, I shifted from teaching writing in a classroom without computers to a **computer-networked** writing lab. While the **Internet** had not yet arrived on campus, we did have a **local area network** that allowed me to set up online writing assignments. We had a one-to-one computer–student ratio, and we held **synchronous chats** in small groups, another strange phenomenon at first. Students sat side by side, silently engaged as never before, rapidly typing messages to fellow students in the same classroom. They did not talk but rather preferred to focus their attention on writing at their computer keyboards.

These experiences of mine occurred during the rapid introduction and evolution of desktop computers in U.S. society. In contrast, today the capabilities and functions of networked computers are commonplace for many students growing up in **networked cultures**. Young people who live in networked cultures are not aware of the vast changes to daily routines that computers and telecommunications networks have introduced in recent history. They may not know that computers were once so large they did not fit on a desktop and were only accessible to a few computer scientists. They have no experiential knowledge of how the world worked prior to the late 1970s when computers first emerged as a household item. A world without the Internet is alien to them. For these students, the first writing tool is often the computer. Their common mode of keeping in touch is online communications. They consider the Internet a living encyclopedia.

Despite the widespread adoption of the Internet in developed societies, many policymakers and educators continue to ask the following:

- How do we know **online literacy learning** is as effective as print-based learning?
- Is students' time spent reading and writing online enabling them to improve in these areas, or does it hinder their literacy abilities?
- Why do teachers need to provide students with online literacy learning opportunities?

I decided to write this book to help teachers of middle-level students know how to respond to these questions. The intended audience is primarily English language arts teachers working with young adolescents, ranging in age from 10 to 15 years,

computer network:
Computers connected by communication lines.

Internet:
Global infrastructure of information and communication networks.

local area network (LAN):
Two or more computers connected by wires or wireless networking to a nearby server.

synchronous chat:
Real-time exchange of online dialogue between multiple participants.

networked culture:
A geographical community connected through Internet access to participants in the global village.

online literacy learning:
Reading, writing, and information research activities that occur via the Internet.

in the middle grades (4–8). Secondary audiences for the book are other middle-level teachers, librarians and media specialists, and teacher preparation faculty interested in literacy development across the curriculum. The focus is on supporting students with learning opportunities that will continue to expand their literacy abilities because it takes more than the basics to be literate citizens of networked cultures.

Although literacy learning on the Internet involves the basic processes of comprehending and writing text, it differs from print-based literacy in significant ways. Text, as defined in this book, includes sources of digital information in print or multimedia formats. Reading and writing text online is highly interactive. Writing becomes more fluent as students engage in online dialogues involving short writing–reading cycles. Online drafting and revising involve a social collaborative process between a writer and his or her immediate audience. Information research becomes a critical reading process useful for sorting through volumes of online texts to find and synthesize reliable data, rather than a memorization of the print encyclopedia. Reading through **hypertexts** or **interactive multimedia** is an active process in which the reader develops an internal narrator who synthesizes meaning and decides which link to follow next and why.

hypertext:
Digital print with hyperlinks readers click on to access other texts.

interactive multimedia:
Related multimodal information that can be presented together with hyperlinks.

The Book's Research Base

The insights in this book stem from my background in the field of educational technology and educational psychology and my program evaluation work during the past decade. Particularly informative to me was a study I organized in the late 1990s to hear firsthand from literacy leaders and classroom teachers about the benefits that accrue from their Internet use with students. I had seen and heard much about the impact of computers on literacy, but the Internet seemed to make a quantum leap over word processing and interactive multimedia CD-ROMs. Literature about the Internet was scarce, so my fellow researchers and I set out to investigate the literacy skills students need to use the Internet effectively, applicable instructional strategies, and the professional development teachers believe they need to capitalize on the Internet's potential for literacy education (McNabb, Hassel, & Steiner, 2002).

These focal points for our study were gleaned from current English language arts and technology learning standards as well as previous research (Becker, 1999; Center for the Improvement of Early Reading Achievement, 1998; Norris & Soloway, 2000), which informed the questions asked during the study. Interviews with well-known literacy researchers and pioneering teachers further shaped questions for an online survey targeting teachers who had significant experience in classroom uses of the Internet. We employed a snowball sampling technique—

which involved gathering referrals to exemplary Internet-using teachers—and found 93 educators in 25 states to participate in the study.

The findings from our study indicate a number of educational benefits that participants associated with using the Internet to support students' literacy development. Teachers said they observed that Internet-based activities make reading enjoyable for students, foster active reading, and facilitate reading fluency. They also stated that Internet use enables students to engage in collaborative discussions and authentic information research experiences that enhance understanding of content. The teachers and researchers emphasized that many conventional reading and writing skills are essential but are just a starting place when using the Internet in the middle grades. Vocabulary development, process writing skills, and comprehension of a variety of texts representing multiple perspectives are typical literacy activities teachers assigned to students online. Our results also indicated that higher order literacy skills, such as organizing information research around a research question, comparing and contrasting, and evaluating and synthesizing information into new and meaningful structures, are important uses of the Internet in literacy education.

We found three primary areas in which the Internet provides curricular benefits. These were information research, writing and publishing, and participating in online learning communities. We (McNabb et al., 2002) also discovered prevalent instructional practices such as

- designing Internet-based activities to help meet the diverse needs of students by engaging them through personal interests;
- customizing the teaching–learning cycle in ways that motivate students to take more responsibility for their learning; and
- fostering self-directed literacy learning habits among students, which researchers and teachers indicated are not only vital to, but also achievable through, Internet-based literacy learning.

The types of practices teachers and literacy researchers emphasized in the study paralleled, in many respects, the principles of effective learning environments, derived from cumulative research about how people learn (see Bransford, Brown, & Cocking, 1999). The more I investigated the dynamics of **networked classrooms**, the more I came to understand how these research-based principles could provide the basis of a framework for organizing literacy opportunities in networked classrooms. That framework is applied throughout this book.

In addition to these findings, the study revealed that most of the participating teachers taught themselves how to use the Internet in literacy education despite the many shifts in literacy conventions and norms and classroom dynamics typically present to those new to teaching in networked classrooms. Despite their

networked classroom:
Environment in which students and teachers use the Internet for educational purposes.

progress in understanding how the Internet can facilitate literacy development, teachers in the study reported high levels of frustration and anxiety because they did not have a guide to help them along the way. They learned by trial and error, and teachers new to using the Internet in literacy education can benefit from their and others' experiences in networked classrooms.

Given the challenging mandates of current educational policies regarding technology, such as the No Child Left Behind Act of 2001 (NCLB; 2002) in the United States, teachers need to understand how the Internet and converging technologies transform learning environments. They must be prepared to provide equitable literacy learning opportunities in networked classrooms.

Overview of the Book

This book is intended to inspire and guide teachers who grapple with how to get started using the Internet in ways that will benefit students' literacy development. From theory to practice, the book presents a research-based framework to guide the design and implementation of Internet-based literacy learning opportunities for students. I took this approach because experience tells me new methods are easier for teachers to understand when they are presented with the theoretical background and how it is applied in practice. Thus, the book begins with an overview of the Internet's short history within education and how the Internet transforms teaching–learning processes related to literacy development. Chapters 3–5 highlight how teachers have taken existing curriculum methods such as literature circles, collaborative research teams, and writing workshops into the online learning environment. Starting with these types of units enables teachers to experience necessary shifts in classroom dynamics and to learn how to scaffold the diverse learning processes of engaged literacy learners.

global village:
Networked cultures around the world connected via the Internet.

virtual communities:
Groups whose members are connected through Internet access for a specific purpose or common interest.

Only after teachers are comfortable with organizing and scaffolding students' online learning opportunities within their own class of students—as exemplified in chapters 3–5—do I recommend they expand their Internet use to include others from the **global village**, as described in chapter 6. Participating in and facilitating online teaching–learning processes takes some practice before teachers are ready to manage learning activities in **virtual communities**. For teachers who are already comfortable teaching in the networked classroom, I have created a four-step design process (see chapter 6) to guide their thinking about how to expand their students' online learning opportunities to include others in the global village.

The practices described in this book align with many of the English language arts and *National Educational Technology Standards for Students* (NETS-S; International Society for Technology in Education [ISTE], 1999). Furthermore, teachers may use the book in professional development settings to meet many of the *National Educational Technology Standards for Teachers* (NETS-T; ISTE, 2002). Each chapter ends with questions to guide discussion among teachers who come together to study the book and share their experiences with teaching in networked classrooms. In addition, a glossary of Internet terminology provides definitions for the technology-related methods discussed in this book. Many of the glossary terms also can be used as keywords when conducting online research for further study about the book's topics and themes.

I encourage readers to engage in professional collaboration when designing and implementing literacy lessons for networked classrooms because they will face many new challenges along the way. In chapters 3, 4, and 5, I demonstrate how the research-based framework applies to actual lessons that facilitate personal ownership for literacy, with an emphasis on reading, information research, and the writing process, respectively. Although these topics are addressed in separate chapters, in actual practice Internet-based literacy activities often draw upon students' reading, writing, and information research abilities in concert. I took an ethnographic approach with Balazs Dibuz, Pamela McDermott, and Bonnie Thurber and Carol Lee to create the descriptions of their curricular units and actual student work in chapters 3, 4, and 5, respectively. Each of the curriculum units highlighted in these chapters illustrates a different way to integrate the Internet into literacy opportunities for middle-level students. As a result, the amount and type of student work and curriculum samples differ for each chapter.

Each chapter has a specific purpose and literacy focus meant to take the guesswork out of using the Internet with middle-level students. Chapter 1 describes a research-based framework to guide teachers' understanding of effective networked classrooms, with attention to the unique characteristics and needs of middle-level students. This chapter includes a discussion of the vital role the Internet plays in literacy education for students growing up to live and work in networked cultures of the 21st century as well as historical and cultural technology trends that influence the current nature of literacy and approaches to learning.

Chapter 2 builds on the theoretical framework by describing in more depth the pedagogical strategies emerging in effective networked classrooms. Successful pedagogy in networked classrooms integrates personalized literacy opportunities within a community of learners. Teachers use scaffolding techniques to adapt their instruction to individual students' learning needs and developmental progress. They manage group learning activities that are highly social by engaging students and others in distributive learning communities. In addition, this chapter describes common learning differences students may present while reading and writing via the Internet and ways to address the differences.

Chapter 3 explains how to apply the pedagogical practices in chapter 2 to foster ownership of literacy in the middle grades, which is fundamental to students' continual development of lifelong literacy habits. The chapter illustrates how online literature circles enhance a unit titled Huck Finn's Journey. The unit cultivates and nurtures students' ownership of literacy through uses of online literature circles. The unit also includes reading informational text students found through online research about the time period of the characters in the book *The Adventures of Huckleberry Finn* (Twain, 1884/2003).

Chapter 4 describes how to apply the essential conditions for effective networked classrooms to online information research activities. The chapter describes how a teacher and school librarian teamed up to teach their students online information research strategies by using a hoax website lesson. Students were presented with a list of websites, some of which were hoaxes and some that were valid. They learned how to locate and critique online information to determine its reliability for a health science project about the human body.

Chapter 5 describes how the Internet can be used to provide a wonderful forum for engaging students in interactive discourse and authentic audience response activities that can help them develop their personal voice and autonomous expression through writing. Highlights from an Online Writers' Workshop include excerpts from online discussions between writing teachers and students as they critique students' developing stories that extend the characters and plots found in the popular novel series about Harry Potter. When students learn to write, constructive feedback can help them develop effective self-monitoring and revision strategies. These aspects of the writing process are shown to illustrate how learning to write can be greatly enhanced through engaging in online writing circles.

Chapter 6 describes a four-step process for designing your own networked classroom to provide students with effective literacy learning opportunities appropriate to those growing up in the global village. The process involves creating an interactive curriculum based on 21st-century literacy standards and students' particular learning needs and identifying benchmarks for progress and appropriate methods of embedded assessment. In addition, the various student and teacher roles within the teaching–learning cycles found in distributive learning communities are discussed.

Finally, chapter 7 is a brief look at pressing concerns and trends facing literacy educators in networked cultures. These include understanding how technology, specifically the Internet, is changing the nature of literacy and the global context for new literacy skills. While many nonnetworked classrooms continue to operate under an outdated system for literacy instruction, a literacy crisis is looming in many high schools. Middle-level teachers are on the forefront to make the changes that can bridge students' basic reading and writing skills with more advanced literacy knowledge and skills necessary to cross the digital divide. The journey toward becoming literate citizens in the global village starts in middle-level networked classrooms with well-prepared teachers.

This book does not cover topics related to setting up an Internet usage policy or how to prepare students with the basic technology operation skills they need to log on and navigate the Internet. Nor does it go into details about how to set up filters or address methods for ensuring the privacy of student work online. Certainly these are important issues when undertaking Internet activities in the classroom. However, there are many different laws, policies, and procedures involved in the governance of children's Internet usage. These are beyond the scope of this book. Readers are encouraged to become informed about their local governance responsibilities when using the Internet with students.

Acknowledgments

I take pause as I write these acknowledgments to friends and colleagues who have inspired me in ways that influenced my writing of this book. There are many more than I can name here. To each with whom I have shared the journey of investigating how the Internet has an impact on classrooms, I express my heartfelt gratitude for your insights.

More specifically, I gratefully acknowledge the people at the North Central Regional Education Laboratory (NCREL) who supported or collaborated on the original study that served as the catalyst for this book, including Gina Burkhardt and Gilbert Valdez, former director and associate director of NCREL, respectively, and consultants Bryan Hassel and Lucy Steiner. Thank you also to the literacy researchers we interviewed for the study and to all the participating teachers we interviewed, observed, and surveyed.

A special thanks to Don Leu, who recommended I submit the original study for publication to the International Reading Association (IRA). Thanks also to Matt Baker, Joan Irwin, the IRA review committee, Elizabeth Hunt, and the IRA editorial staff for their feedback and guidance as I developed the manuscript.

Among informal reviewers was my mother, Janet, to whom I faxed drafts of this manuscript while it was under development. I thank her for the thoughtful reflection and commentary as well as skillful editing suggestions.

I thank my contributing authors, their coteachers, and their students for sharing their work with the readers of this book. Balazs Dibuz, a language arts and social studies teacher at Quest Academy in Palatine, Illinois, teaches with colleague Andrew Shilhanek the Huck Finn's Journey unit featured in chapter 3. Pamela A. McDermott, a library information specialist at Glen Crest Middle School in Glen Ellyn, Illinois, teaches with Mary Fran McBreen the Understanding Human Body Systems unit featured in chapter 4. Bonnie Thurber, who is responsible for Programs, Professional Development, and Online Projects at the Northwestern University Collaboratory Project in Evanston, Illinois, and educational consultant

Carol Ann Lee teach the Online Writers' Workshop featured in chapter 5 for Northwestern's Center for Talent Development. A special thanks to Bonnie also for her involvement as a participant in the original study that shaped the premise for this book (see McNabb et al., 2002) and for helping me recruit Balazs Dibuz and Carol Ann Lee.

My perspective about the characteristics of effective networked classrooms has been influenced by my involvement with the Preparing Tomorrow's Teachers to Use Technology (PT3) grant programs in several ways. I thank all those who voiced informed opinions about the educational value of information and communication technology while I was serving on the national committee developing the NETS-T (ISTE, 2002), which was supported by the PT3 grant program. I gratefully acknowledge the PT3 Vision Quest think tank, a group with whom I rigorously debated the impact of the Internet on dynamics of teaching, learning, and assessment. In particular, I would like to express my gratitude to two PT3 Vision Quest members: Tom Carroll, past director for the PT3 grant program, and John Bransford, lead author of the *How People Learn* report (Bransford, Brown, & Cocking, 1999), who invited me to continue our collaboration through the PT3 How People Learn grant at Vanderbilt University during 2002–2003. The works of both of these men and discussions I have shared with them and the PT3 community helped shape my understanding about the important influence the Internet has and will continue to have on learning environments in the 21st century.

Last, but not least, I gratefully acknowledge the many administrators, teachers, and students whom I have observed, assessed, and interviewed during my program evaluation work with schools implementing the Internet into classrooms. Their candor about accomplishments and consequences of teaching and learning in networked classrooms has taught me much about what works and why.

Much has gone into the writing of this book. Thank you all!

Mary L. McNabb
mlmcnabb@learningauge.org
www.LearninGauge.org

CHAPTER 1

Exploring the Internet in Literacy Learning

Understanding the role the **Internet** can play in literacy development involves understanding historical connections between literacy, technology, and culture. Many cultural forces affect the nature of literacy, and the Internet is no exception. Those with access to the Internet use it daily at home, at the library, and at work for a variety of social, economic, and educational purposes (Nie & Erbing, 2000). According to the Silicon Valley Cultures Project, the networking capacity of the Internet affects the nature of cultural activities, relationships, roles and norms, processes, and information resources in a much more profound way than isolated uses of technologies (English-Lueck, 1998). The rapid expansion and adoption of the Internet into daily routines at home, at work, and for leisure make it a transformative global force. And, because the Internet is text-based, the reading and writing demands it generates are immense.

Educators and policymakers around the world are seeking to harness the transformative power of the Internet for educational purposes. A computer scientist, Sugata Mitra, conducted a now-famous study known as the *Hole in the Wall Experiment* (Judge, 2000). This study was a naturalistic observation of children living in poor conditions on the streets of Delhi, India. Mitra provided the street children with free access to a computer with a high-speed Internet connection, which appeared through a hole in the wall of his office building. He put a camera in a tree and observed the children's natural curiosity. Within days they had taught themselves the rudiments of computer use and Internet **surfing**.

Mitra found that the most avid users of the Internet were children ages 6 to 12 who had at least some basic literacy education. He repeated the study with rural children and had similar findings. A key component of the children's learning was collaboration among themselves to satisfy their curiosity. Mitra concluded from his observations of the children's learning approach that teachers need to be trained in noninvasive teaching techniques for guiding children's use of the Internet that motivate rather than control *how* children learn.

Internet:
Global infrastructure of information and communication networks.

surf:
To browse information on the Web leisurely.

Noninvasive teaching techniques are learner-centered methods teachers use to adapt their instruction to students' prior knowledge, interests, and learning styles in ways that move students beyond what they can do on their own. The children Mitra observed spent time teaching themselves how to surf the **World Wide Web**, but the literacy challenge in the middle grades is more about teaching students how to conduct a **digital search** or how to read information on the Web critically to make meaning. It is about fostering students' personal and social comprehension of **hypertexts**, helping them find and express their voices within supportive learning communities, and using the Internet to foster their ownership of literacy—to motivate them to make sense of and contribute to the **global village** in which they live.

World Wide Web:

Public portion of the Internet's online information resources.

digital search:

Strategic use of online search engines, indexes, and directories.

hypertext:

Digital print with hyperlinks readers click on to access other texts.

global village:

Networked cultures around the world connected via the Internet.

computer network:

Computers connected by communication lines.

The Global Village Network

The Internet is an open-ended architecture that webs and weaves together cultures around the globe. Its design today still reflects its origin founded on an underlying philosophy of free speech and localized publishing. Agre (1999) explains that the Internet was originally designed for the scientific community. As a result, its fundamental characteristic of open-endedness mirrors that community's high capacity for self-regulation, reflection, interactive discourse, and data warehousing. In more recent years, commerce, news, and entertainment have expanded the Internet's capacity and population of users.

The Internet consists of hundreds of millions of interconnected **computer networks**, which together house a collection of information and human resources beyond the imaginings of yesteryear. One of the cumulative effects of the Internet, within the past 10 years, has been a leveling of access to learning opportunities for new knowledge and skills necessary to participate in 21st-century economies (Friedman, 2005). With the amount of information and human networking capacity of the Internet growing exponentially every day, its influence on academic and lifelong learning will continue to increase (Lockard & Abrams, 2004).

In 2001, technological advances made it possible to send more information in one second than could be sent over the entire Internet during one month in 1997 (Fukuda-Parr & Birdsall, 2001). The cost of transmitting information also has fallen drastically. For example, a person with Internet access can now e-mail a 40-page document from Chile to Kenya for no cost. It arrives almost instantly. Likewise, someone in Siberia can post a webpage that is quickly accessible to someone in Chicago. Through use of the Internet, those in remote areas of the world can access the same online resources as those in more developed, affluent areas. During 2002, for example, war-torn Afghanistan opened its country's first

Internet connection via a satellite system connected to a computer in the library at Kabul University (Hadlow, 2002). The university's rector explained that

> the University was badly affected by 23 years of war, with most of the library books and other documents being destroyed. We cannot replace all the books, but now we can look on the Internet to read materials from all over the world. (¶ 2)

Launching the Internet at this once isolated university has far-reaching impacts on its staff and students. They now have the ability to converse with people in other **networked cultures** and to access updated resources that can shed new light on knowledge stored in their human memory. The Internet will undoubtedly confront them, as it does everyone, with new literacy challenges. Those in remote areas of the global village will need to acquire the same skills as those in metropolitan cities in order to participate in cultural activities involving online information and communication.

Ongoing Challenges for Literacy Learning

Because the Internet is a dynamic environment that rapidly changes and expands, literacy learning is ongoing in the global village. It requires that we be able to transfer and adapt our reading and writing skills within a variety of social contexts and text formats. We need to be astute at evaluating the credibility of online resources and skillful at applying audience awareness to **real-time authoring**. As online readers, we also need to think critically about how we navigate through the multiple layers of meaning on a single screen and make choices about which link to click next. We each chart our own unique course for meaning making. We make inferential leaps about unclear associations between nodes of information based on our prior knowledge. In essence, we create a narrative in our minds to keep ourselves from getting lost in thought and purpose. We click forward to create text structures more easily found in print and depend upon our internal narrator to provide a pattern for decoding the meaning of **multisequential** texts. Online, there is no ending to the story, so we seek to create our own. We then log off and back on to create a new narrative, not knowing how to re-create the one from yesterday's reading of the Web.

In its relatively short history as a cultural presence, the Internet has profoundly influenced literacy norms and language conventions in networked cultures. Terms such as hypertext, **synchronous chats**, **blogs**, and **emoticons** that are finding their way into everyday vocabularies are representative of this trend. Seamless convergence of **digital authoring tools** and telecommunications through the Internet has facilitated cultural shifts in literacy on many levels (Cognition and Technology Group at Vanderbilt, 1997; Riel & Harasim, 1994;

networked culture:
A geographical community connected through Internet access to participants in the global village.

real-time authoring:
The act of writing original texts for a live audience.

multisequential:
Allows for diverse reading options in a single hypertext.

synchronous chat:
Real-time exchange of online dialogue between multiple participants.

blog:
A Web log with dated entries that functions as an online journal.

emoticon:
A group of keyboard characters used to express emotion.

digital authoring tools:
Software for creating hypertexts, interactive multimedia, or word-processing documents.

virtual communities:
Groups whose
members are
connected through
Internet access for a
specific purpose or
common interest.

Romiszowski, 1997). New literacy skills are needed to access online databases of information and to participate in **virtual communities** organized online around common interests. In addition, online reading and writing tasks require that we apply knowledge of media grammars and global literary conventions. The list of literacy skills needed for successful participation in the global village shifts as Internet functions and norms change.

The Internet reminds us that the nature of literacy tends to be culturally bound. Leu and Kinzer (2000) explain the powerful influence cultural forces have on the nature of literacy: "Ultimately, the forms and functions of literacy as well as literacy instruction itself are largely determined by the cultural forces at work within any society" (p. 111). Literacy researchers who reflect on the influence of technology on literacy conclude that "technology has frequently played a dominant role in defining what reading and writing skills have been considered important, as well as how and to whom they were taught" (Reinking & Bridwell-Bowles, 1996, p. 310). The Internet's influence on the literacy skills people use to access resources and communicate information has been astounding in recent history.

The Internet's Impact on Middle-Level Literacy Development

Fifteen years ago, the most avid Internet users were researchers and scientists. Today, preteens and adolescents are among the most avid user groups. They use the Internet for socializing, shopping, planning, learning, playing games, and listening to music. Tapscott (1998) claims that through the use of digital media, today's youths "are a force for social transformation" (p. 2). Those who have acquired adequate reading and writing abilities for online learning teach themselves about serious global problems and collaborate on finding solutions. They use their leisure time to participate in online social chats, special interest clubs, and in-depth investigations empowering them to change society. They create their own symbol systems and govern themselves by generating and enforcing strong codes of online conduct.

Tapscott (1998) shows that Internet use has noteworthy impacts on children's development. In his synopsis of the "Internet Generation" of U.S. children who were between the ages of 2 and 22 before the millennium, he wrote,

> Child development is concerned with the evolution of motor skills, language skills, and social skills. It also involves the development of cognition, intelligence, reasoning, personality, and, through adolescence the creation of autonomy, a sense of the self and values.... When children control their media, rather than passively observe, they develop faster.... [C]hildren without access to the new media [online] will be developmentally disadvantaged. (p. 7)

One thing clear from Tapscott's work is that the Internet is a powerful force in the lives of the young people who use it regularly. Teachers who successfully integrate the Internet into their classrooms capitalize on students' intrinsic motivation for engaging in online activities, while fostering their literacy development at an accelerated pace.

Internet use can particularly help facilitate age-appropriate literacy development for middle-level students. Students in the middle grades are in transition from childhood to young adulthood. Their experiences will shape their habits of mind for the future, so the time is optimal for them to learn how to take ownership of their literacy, to build their own vocabulary, and to express their personal perspectives in relation to the multiple perspectives of others. There also is a strong connection between literacy development and identity. According to Moore, Bean, Birdyshaw, and Rycik (1999), "Reading difficulties do not occur in a vacuum. Adolescents' personal identities, academic achievement, and future aspirations mix with ongoing difficulties with reading" (p. 8).

During young adolescence, students' interactions with others shape their understanding of self and value within a community. In *This We Believe: Successful Schools for Young Adolescents* (National Middle School Association [NMSA], 2003b), experts explain that young adolescent students have a strong need for approval from trustworthy peers and at the same time need supportive boundaries from caring adults. Although they seek to be in meaningful relationships with adults, they also are inquisitive and often challenge adults' authority in order to observe their responses. In addition, students in the middle grades often appear disinterested in academics but usually are curious about the world around them. They are inclined to explore a wide range of intellectual pursuits, few of which are sustained.

On the Internet, students can explore the world and their relationship to it through literacy events that support their developing autonomies, personal identities, and social selves. Personal expression and perspective sharing are attributes of literacy that tie in to students' emerging identities as lifelong learners and knowledgeable contributors to society. Online, students can benefit from having more than one expert in their learning circle: They learn to no longer rely on a teacher as their sole source of correctness. Within a learning community, they are challenged to take responsibility for their own insights and develop self-expression.

The literacy learning challenges at the middle level differ quite a bit from the challenges of learning the basics for reading and writing at the elementary level. By the time students reach the middle grades, they are expected to read and write fluently at grade level and to be able to enjoy the benefits of taking ownership of their literacy. They also need to know how to activate self-monitoring strategies such as rereading, questioning, and word identification when their comprehension begins to break down (International Reading Association [IRA] & National Association for the Education of Young Children, 1998). They are expected to possess basic skills for researching and writing on a variety of topics to suit their intended purposes and audiences.

In order to meet and exceed these expectations, young adolescents need a literacy learning environment that allows them to apply their basic literacy skills in ways that reinforce their literacy development and challenge it to grow. They need to increase their comprehension fluency with a broad spectrum of texts and to expand their vocabulary continually. They need feedback from authentic audiences about their writing and guidance from writing mentors to advance their writing skills. With its unlimited choices for reading, writing, and interacting with others, the Internet offers powerful literacy venues for middle-level students.

Literacy acts online require students to write fluently with self-expression and to read with a critic's eye. Online writing often results in immediate audience responses, which prompts students to respond with revisions or to take a critical stand. According to Tapscott (1998), "Time spent on the Internet is not passive time, it's active time. It's reading time. It's investigation time. It's skill development and problem-solving time. It's time analyzing, evaluating. It's composing your thoughts time. It's writing time" (p. 8). However, the open-ended nature of the Internet also poses a possible stumbling block for students whose autonomous thinking and ownership of literacy are still emerging. Without the appropriate guidance, students' literacy development may flounder rather than flourish in the **networked classroom**. Thus, the purpose of this book is to empower teachers with the knowledge and skills necessary to ensure their networked classrooms are effective learning environments for supporting their students' literacy development in the 21st century.

networked classroom:
Environment in which students and teachers use the Internet for educational purposes.

Expectations For Effective Learning Environments

The online learning environment that students seek of their own accord after school is very different from a nonnetworked classroom. In the online environment, everyone has a voice, while in nonnetworked classrooms, only a few typically do. Online, students can forge their own reading path to comprehend concepts and events, but in many nonnetworked classrooms, teachers often dispense information according to a logical sequence determined by curriculum committees. In contrast, teachers who use an interactive curriculum provide students with learning resources that facilitate literacy development in ways unobtainable when using a print-based curriculum. The shifts in classroom dynamics associated with these changes may overwhelm teachers at first.

When the Internet comes into the classroom, teachers may feel displaced because classroom roles, instructional practices, and assessment needs often shift and some educational policies no longer fit (McNabb, 2001). As a result of these changes, educational policymakers have launched a global movement to define the accountability and assessment policies for governing uses of the Internet in schools (Leu, 2000). Literacy issues that teachers and policymakers are grappling with include how best to manage quality control of online information resources, how to measure comprehension of hypertext, and how to safely provide students access to learning communities beyond the school walls. The more teachers understand dynamics in networked classrooms, the more they will be able to effectively integrate the Internet in ways that shape new policy initiatives governing educational uses of the Internet.

Figure 1 illustrates a framework for organizing networked classrooms using proximal instruction that supports learner control, an interactive curriculum that fosters ownership of literacy, and embedded assessments that provide formative feedback for individual students within a distributive community of literacy

FIGURE 1
Characteristics of Effective Learning Opportunities in Networked Classrooms

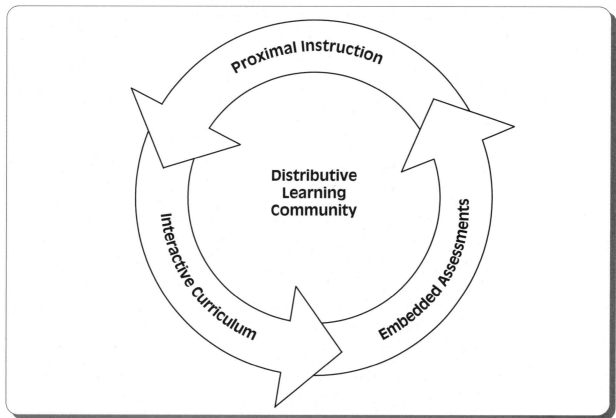

learners. The term *proximal instruction* refers to a learner-centered pedagogical method teachers use to scaffold students' literacy development along a continuum aligned to standards. The framework builds on findings about research-based characteristics of effective learning environments as the basis for describing the pedagogy, curriculum, and assessments appropriate for networked classrooms. The research evidence for the framework comes from the learning sciences' interdisciplinary study of learning and teaching through real-world settings. The learning sciences include disciplines such as education, cognitive science, sociology, information sciences, and instructional design. The research basis for the framework in Figure 1 is summarized below and further described and applied throughout this book as a theoretical approach to designing and managing the teaching–learning process in networked classrooms.

A recent global study that investigated the use of information and communication technology in the educational systems of 28 countries confirms that the educational effectiveness of the Internet often depends on pedagogical practices in the networked classroom (Kozma, 2003). We also know from cumulative research findings spanning 30 years in the learning sciences that effective learning environments have four primary characteristics. These are (1) community centeredness, (2) learner centeredness, (3) assessment centeredness, and (4) knowledge centeredness (Bransford et al., 1999).

Community Centeredness

Highly social learning environments are *community centered*, a term that refers to practices that encourage participation among everyone in a classroom. Community provides students with a sense of belonging and encourages them to think creatively and critically. Within viable learning communities, students can pose alternative viewpoints and learn from their mistakes without fear of punitive consequences (Bransford et al., 1999).

Facilitating students' literacy development is a complex undertaking in any learning environment. In networked classrooms, dynamics shift from teacher-led learning activities to distributive learning community activities. In distributive learning communities, students begin to feel secure knowing that everyone has the right to participate. They voluntarily respond to their perceived obligation to abide by rules of engagement established for the learning community. Their understanding about learning community norms and rules of engagement is important because students are contributing to one another's development. Once secure, students can explore their literacy development in personalized ways. They feel free to probe their peers and teachers. They often become actively engaged in dialogue with professionals and community members to generate a collective understanding of a subject or problem under study. Peer mentoring may happen spontaneously. Effective distributive learning communities nurture students' development and achievement by providing a comfortable environment for them to ask questions, share their misconceptions, and show their vulnerability. Students who participate in learning communities tend to gain awareness of not only their achievements but also their unique learning styles and needs.

Learner Centeredness

Effective literacy environments also provide all students with opportunities to learn. Traditionally, the concept of an opportunity to learn has referred to the ethical practice of providing equitable conditions within a classroom. A more contemporary understanding is that an opportunity to learn for one student may not meet the developmental needs of another student in the same group. Lessons that help students build on their prior knowledge and personal interests for reading and writing are *learner centered*. **Online literacy learning** experiences tend to be learner centered because digital texts provide students with a high degree of learner control (Au, 1997; Kamil, Intrator, & Kim, 2000; J.M. Wood, 2000). Learner control is evident in the different reading paths students may take on an assigned website, for example. Effective Internet-using teachers design learner-centered lessons that provide students with valid options in online resources so they can forge their own learning paths that build on their existing literacy strengths and cultural values.

online literacy learning: Reading, writing, and information research activities that occur via the Internet.

Research also tells us that students learn using different styles, at different paces, and with different levels of motivation that affect their achievement (e.g., American Psychological Association [APA] Task Force on Psychology in Education, 1993; APA Work Group of the Board of Educational Affairs, 1997; Bransford et al., 1999; Gardner, 1993). The arrival of the Internet in schools challenges teachers to develop new teaching methods that apply learner-centered strategies aligned with differences among students. Leu and Kinzer (2000) predict,

> Now, literacy instruction at all levels—pre-K through college—means incorporating a much more authentic and learner-centered approach. In the future, with the aid of interactive, multimedia technologies, it will come to mean even more learner-based instruction, with learners controlling their own destinations to achieving their goals. (p. 123)

The effectiveness of students' learner control is often dependent on how well teachers address personal learner needs among diverse students within a distributive learning community. Instructional decisions about curriculum designs to accommodate a range in student needs are best grounded in timely data about students' literacy progress.

Assessment Centeredness

Teachers will be hard pressed to manage learner-centered opportunities for all students within a distributive learning community unless they engage in *assessment-centered* practices. In effective learning environments, assessments are primarily formative in nature and provide students opportunities for feedback and revision (Bransford et al., 1999). Frequent cycles of assessment, feedback, and revision take time, which often presents a major impediment for teachers. However, online assessment tools can provide powerful ways for embedding assessments into students' learning processes that return results in an efficient, timely manner.

Participants in an online learning community also are valuable sources of formative assessment feedback. Teachers who are assessment centered typically include students in decisions about how the students are assessed. Teachers who select or design assessments that yield formative feedback related to literacy benchmarks can make timely use of data to inform their instructional decisions. In classrooms that are assessment centered, students have opportunities to visualize their thinking in concrete formats so they can reflect on and correct errors or misconceptions (Bransford et al., 1999). Formative assessments enable students to self-organize and self-monitor their literacy learning progress based on constructive feedback.

Knowledge Centeredness

Effective learning environments also are *knowledge centered* (Bransford et al., 1999). Bransford (2001) states,

> Being knowledge-centered involves looking at the world in which people will eventually operate and then designing learning opportunities by working backward from that perspective. Being knowledge-centered also involves a serious examination of how to help students learn with understanding rather than only memorizing. This can help students organize and facilitate subsequent transfer [of their learning]. (¶ 6)

Teachers who focus classroom activities solely on transmitting knowledge often devalue or dismiss students' questions that expose their lack of understanding, which results in disadvantages to those students. Traditionally, when a student does not know something, doors close to future learning opportunities for that student. But in a knowledge-centered learning environment, a student's lack of knowing is valued as the basis for making decisions about how to adapt instruction to resolve students' misconceptions. A knowledge-centered approach, combined with embedded assessments and learner-centered options within a distributive community, increases the likelihood that learners can organize their knowledge, skills, and attitudes in ways that support transfer of what is learned in one context to other novel contexts. Bransford and Schwartz (1999) call this preparing people for future learning, which implies they can apply and adapt their prior knowledge in ways that facilitate further learning from new circumstances.

In effective networked classrooms, teachers design and implement interactive curricula that motivate students to enjoy tasks involving writing for real audiences, acquiring new vocabularies, and critically researching and reading informational text or literature. When students have opportunities to engage in reading and writing assignments that connect with their strengths and present interesting challenges to their preconceptions, they will be motivated to participate. When students receive frequent and useful feedback that can guide their writing progress, that is motivating. In addition, students who are able to contribute as valued participants in a vibrant literacy community often find reading and writing exciting.

Conclusion

In today's global village, the Internet has become a significant literacy landscape. Information and communication technologies, converging on the Internet, expand literacy demands beyond narrative print to complex hypertext resources and online communities. Its network of cultures, people, and information expands students' resources beyond textbooks and trade books and provides a rich environment for literacy learning. Online, students are exposed to a plurality of literacy norms and social contexts that challenge their literacy development in ways that ask teachers to think anew about their classroom practices.

Historically, classroom teachers sent students to a computer lab while they took time out from teaching to plan their next lesson or to grade papers. Students during computer time were under the supervision of the computer teacher. Today, technology integration is occurring more directly in classrooms. Portable hand-held devices that have **wireless** Internet connections now make it feasible for classrooms to become networked computing labs. This trend is expected to grow. Access to **portable technology** connected to the Internet via a wireless network is less expensive for schools than desktop computer labs run by additional teaching staff. As a result, classroom teachers are facing a growing pressure to become active users of technology and digital curricula. To succeed, teachers are acquiring new pedagogical strategies applicable to networked classrooms, which call for more, not less, teacher monitoring of students' literacy learning processes. Chapter 2 describes the pedagogy emerging in networked classrooms to help teachers conquer the new challenges they will encounter while facilitating online literacy opportunities for students in the middle grades.

wireless:
Transmission of information without cables or cords.

portable technology:
Small technology devices that are easily transported.

GUIDING QUESTIONS FOR DISCUSSION

1. What are the cultural influences of the Internet on literacy in the global village?

2. What are the key characteristics of the Internet that particularly support young adolescents' literacy development?

3. How can research findings about effective learning environments inform networked classroom practices?

4. How do the literacy opportunities available on the Internet compare to those in nonnetworked classrooms?

CHAPTER 2

The Pedagogy of Distributive Learning Communities

While sitting in a **networked classroom**, I recently observed seventh-grade students using laptops to complete a literacy assignment. The energy level in the room was amazing, and the students seemed to be highly engaged. When I took a closer look over students' shoulders to view their online work, I discovered a wide variance in how students approached the assigned task. Some were working independently with a word-processing program and **Internet browser** open. They toggled between windows to read a website and then cut and paste text from the **World Wide Web** into their notes file. Some had recruited a peer group and were actively seeking consultation. Others were playing commercial games or simply clicking aimlessly as they **surfed** the Web. During this activity, the teacher sat in the back of the room grading papers. She appeared altogether unaware of her students' diverse learning performance and missed the opportunity to scaffold their literacy development in meaningful ways.

This teacher's approach to designing literacy learning opportunities for students on the World Wide Web was to assign all students an independent reading task. Research indicates, however, that sustained silent reading without guidance or scaffolding does not have significant positive impacts on students' academic progress (National Institute of Child Health and Human Development [NICHD], 2000; Paul, 1996). Paul investigated the impact of giving students time to read in class and found that when the literacy environment supports students developmentally there is a strong positive correlation with students' overall academic achievement measured by the National Assessment of Educational Progress (NAEP). However, Paul's research shows that most reading growth at the middle level occurs when students are given 60 minutes a day for independent reading that includes guidance from teachers on a personal basis. Although the research pertains to print-based curricula, these findings have important implications for the pedagogy of networked classrooms.

networked classroom: Environment in which students and teachers use the Internet for educational purposes.

Internet: Global infrastructure of information and communication networks.

browser: An online interface used to access and read hypertext and interactive multimedia housed on the World Wide Web.

World Wide Web: Public portion of the Internet's online information resources.

surf: To browse information on the Web leisurely.

In networked classrooms, it is imperative that teachers strike a balance between allowing students to independently read highly interactive and often open-ended curriculum resources online and scaffolding their reading. Integrating the Internet into classrooms is most difficult for teachers whose pedagogy is aimed at controlling how students access content and interact with others. Online literacy assignments are often collaborative and occur in the context of distributive learning communities. Guiding rather than controlling young adolescents' literacy acts is a desirable approach to literacy learning because it fosters their ownership of literacy development in the context of the **global village**. This makes the Internet a natural fit with middle-level curricular goals for relevant, challenging, integrative, and exploratory curriculum designs (NMSA, 2003b). Some students may thrive in the networked classroom with little guidance, while others may need intense scaffolding to foster their literacy development. This chapter describes the characteristics of pedagogy emerging in distributive learning communities and the important role teachers play in scaffolding the literacy development of diverse students.

global village:
Networked cultures around the world connected via the Internet.

Characteristics of Proximal Instruction

Proximal instruction is a term I coined while conducting an in-depth study of teachers' monitoring strategies while teaching in networked classrooms (McNabb, 1996). The term refers to a learner-centered pedagogical method that teachers use to scaffold students' literacy development along a continuum aligned to standards. During proximal instruction, teachers adapt their interactions with students to address the variance in students' cognitive ability to complete assigned literacy tasks (McNabb, 1996; McNabb & Smith, 1998). Proximal instruction promotes cognitive development of learners' autonomous literacy skills. It also serves to motivate students in ways that foster ownership of literacy. Both autonomy and motivation are paramount factors for successful learning with an interactive curriculum—which gives students much more control over their literacy activities than a print-based curriculum.

Online, students become active readers and writers. Their individual literacy abilities and learning differences become apparent. Their unique literacy struggles, perhaps once latent or undetectable to the teacher, come to the foreground (McNabb, 1996). Proximal instruction strategies provide teachers with ways to strike a balance between learner autonomy and accountability to learning standards. Adapting instruction to the needs of individual students is a key characteristic of proximal instruction. Such an approach is consistent with current learning theory. When it comes to reading, "research makes it very clear that there is no single instructional program or method that is effective in teaching all children to read" (IRA, 2002). An assignment for one student may not be adequate for another; proximal instruction provides a systematic method for adjusting learning opportunities based on student diversity.

Proximal instruction is a learner-centered approach that supports highly social and interactive curricular activities, which are indicative of networked classrooms (Garner & Gillingham, 1998; Kozma, 2003; Leu & Kinzer, 2000; McNabb et al., 2002). Teachers who are learner centered adapt their instruction to address students' diversity in the *zone of proximal development* (Vygotsky, 1934/1978). Vygotsky defined the zone of proximal development as the student's developmental level between independent problem solving and a higher level of development attainable with "guidance or in collaboration with more capable peers" (p. 86). Vygotsky described the role of the adult in the child's development as a

> more competent person [who] collaborates with a child to help him move from where he is now to where he can be with help. This person accomplishes this feat by means of prompts, clues, modeling, explanation, leading questions, discussion, joint participation, encouragement, control of the child's [or student's] attention, and so on. (as cited in Miller, 1993, p. 379)

Vygotskian research demonstrates that interactions between the child and the more competent person or peer awaken "a variety of internal developmental processes" that occur only in the context of such social interactions (as cited in Miller, 1993, p. 379).

I have observed examples of such interaction in a number of networked classrooms in high-poverty, high-achievement school settings known for sustaining significant academic improvements across multiple years. In these settings, the young adolescent students had **wireless** laptops for a one-to-one student–computer ratio, and teachers were able to watch students' online activities through a **real-time** curriculum and assessment management system. Participating teachers routinely gave students a quiz embedded into a lesson and could view and record students' responses as they typed. The teachers also were able to monitor who was participating, who was not responding, and who was correctly or incorrectly answering the questions. Students voluntarily used **instant messaging** to ask their teachers for clarification to assessment questions or help for in-class assignments when they needed it. Teachers responded to students on an individual basis using instant messaging, which reduced interruptions in the face-to-face classroom for other students. As a result, student engagement increased.

Research indicates that when student engagement increases, so does the likelihood for transfer of learning from one context to other contexts beyond a specific learning task (Bransford et al., 1999). In the networked classrooms described, teachers routinely monitored, diagnosed, and scaffolded each

wireless:
Transmission of information without cables or cords.

real time:
Live interactions online such as in synchronous chats.

instant messaging:
One-on-one online dialogue in real time.

student's developmental level using online quizzes and minilessons to review, reteach, or accelerate the curriculum accordingly. In essence, this is proximal instruction in action. Teachers in these schools routinely used the Internet to help them monitor student progress and adapted their instruction to the proximal development levels of individual students. As a result, they were successful at accelerating the literacy development of the young adolescents who had previously experienced the detrimental impacts of poverty on their literacy achievement (McNabb, 2004).

Data-Driven Decisions

Complex learning environments, such as the one just described, require teachers to make many decisions throughout the day (Guillaume, 2000). The teachers discussed were successful because the Internet-based application they used allowed them to monitor students' learning and to respond to students' unique instructional needs online without disrupting other students in the room. I have met other teachers who, instead of monitoring students' learning processes, routinely base their instructional decisions on philosophical beliefs about teaching rather than on timely and reliable data about their students' progress toward meeting standards. This approach to teaching has a fundamental flaw. Without reliable and timely student learning data, teachers are prone to make biased decisions about the effectiveness of their teaching and about individuals or groups of students (Bandura, 1986; Haney, Lumpe, Czerniak, & Egan, 2002).

The Internet and converging technologies now make it possible to assess students' learning regularly. Technology-supported assessments generate real-time data to inform teachers' decision-making process. Without the assistance of technology, constructing and conducting frequent classroom assessments can be impractical. In networked classrooms, teachers can access timely data that enables them to know what students really know. Without such data, teachers may assume that some students are not capable of learning as well as others and sort students based on false presumptions (Serim & Salpeter, 2003). In the networked classroom, in which students have many more options and resources, their learning may take unconventional pathways to proficiency. Teachers who embed formative assessments into their teaching routines obtain the types of data necessary for scaffolding students' literacy development in ways appropriate for addressing differences among learners.

Wiggins (1993) explains that effective instruction provides frequent and clear information to students about their performance and how it compares with an exemplary standard. Instructive feedback indicates consequences of good and poor performance, supplies information to help students troubleshoot their own performance, and also facilitates continuous learning. Instructive feedback is the substance of proximal instruction strategies.

Strategies for Scaffolding Learner Control

Teachers who take a proximal instruction approach use a variety of strategies to scaffold students' learning experiences. They look for discrepancies between students' performance and academic benchmarks. They recognize when students are overly frustrated or taking risks that lead them astray and intervene to demonstrate the optimum way to complete a task only after a student shows an inability to progress further on his or her own. Their interactions with students provide them with valuable evidence about what students do and do not know. They recognize that when students do not know how to perform a task or answer a question in class, the nature of their misconceptions provides the foundation for future teaching. They understand that there is a time for telling, a time for observing, a time for questioning, and a time for demonstrating.

Teachers who practice proximal instruction guide literacy activities with the goal of fostering students' ability to perform assigned reading and writing tasks independently. They adapt their instruction according to students' prior independent performance, which they have observed and monitored. For example, I found that teachers use two types of proximal instruction strategies during literacy instruction in networked classrooms: *descriptive strategies* and *prescriptive strategies* (McNabb, 1996; McNabb & Smith, 1998). Teachers use descriptive strategies, which are characterized by a variety of open-ended cues, to elicit reflective and evaluative responses from students, as long as the students are able to self-evaluate and progress in their learning. Examples of descriptive strategies described in McNabb (1996) include

- *exploring* or *probing* a variety of alternative methods or perspectives;
- *mirroring* back to the student his or her own thinking process through verbal reiteration;
- *negotiating* the method for accomplishing a task or the meaning of a text;
- *prompting* students to think in depth about their ideas and the language they are using to express those ideas within an argumentative context;
- *simulating* contexts for learning that resemble situations calling for autonomous skill performance, in other words, counter argumentation techniques, Socratic dialogue, and authentic reading and writing tasks. (p. 212)

When students do not respond favorably to descriptive strategies, teachers switch to prescriptive strategies, which are characterized by close-ended comments, direct instruction, and explicit demonstrations. Teachers use prescriptive strategies to model solutions to students' literacy learning problems until they are able to elicit imitative responses from students. Examples of prescriptive strategies described in McNabb (1996) include

- *explaining* or *elaborating* on the purposes, beliefs, procedures, rules, and/or conceptual substance of reading and writing tasks;

- *goal setting* to make explicit the characteristics of a task and/or the subcomponents of the task that act as benchmarks of achievement;
- *modeling* or *demonstrating* to students how a given task may be accomplished;
- *suggesting* specific solutions to a literacy learning problem. (p. 212)

Proximal instruction strategies help develop students' self-regulatory learning abilities, which enable students "to plan, monitor success, and correct errors when appropriate" through the executive control of their own performance (Bransford et al., 1999, p. 85). These types of strategies enable teachers to foster learner control and autonomous thinking among students (McNabb, 1996). Students who take control of their literacy learning are taking ownership of their literacy. They begin managing their own literacy development and tend to show more achievement gains than those who do not. Au and Raphael (2000) explain,

> Students with ownership understand the personal aspects of literacy, which leads to positive attitudes about literacy and habits of using literacy in everyday life for their own purposes. There is a reciprocal relationship between ownership of and proficiency with literacy. (p. 178)

Successful proximal instruction decisions are based on observations and data from assessments embedded into students' real-time literacy performance. During proximal instruction, teachers use the array of strategies to manage diversity among students and to keep all students progressing in their literacy development.

Addressing Learner Diversity

Variance among students tends to intensify in the middle grades as young adolescents undergo rapid spurts of growth and personal development at varying rates (NMSA, 2003b). Their differences may be great or small depending on personal attributes related to cognitive processes, personal motivations, and prior literacy knowledge. During proximal instruction, teachers need to be aware of common differences in students' cognitive processes observable during online reading, information research, and writing. These literacy activities engage brain functions responsible for language, metacognition, memory, attention, and spatial processing. For example, metacognitive monitoring during reading and writing can be hindered by attention or memory deficits aggravated by the intense interactivity of **hypertext** and **synchronous chats**. Even students who do not struggle with reading and writing in the print-based curriculum may need more guidance when engaging in reading or writing activities online. Student learning problems can be more prevalent in the networked classroom because the Internet is an open-ended environment in which students must learn how to self-regulate

hypertext:
Digital print with hyperlinks readers click on to access other texts.

synchronous chat:
Real-time exchange of online dialogue between multiple participants.

their learning. Effective teachers in networked classrooms intervene directly in students' online literacy acts in order to scaffold their literacy development.

Teachers who take a proximal instruction approach to teaching in networked classrooms allow students to perform at their own pace, which also facilitates ownership of literacy. They design curricula that have options for students. They often will use digital resources to provide those options, which also assists students in adapting assignments to their personal zones of proximal development. In contrast, for teachers in traditional classrooms without Internet access, it may not be as feasible to adapt learning opportunities for every student. However, the networked classroom opens new possibilities for addressing learner differences.

If learner differences are not addressed, teachers may actually create a dysfunctional learning environment in which some students are unable to progress. In essence, some students become learning disabled when their different needs go unaddressed in the classroom (Levine, 2002). Differences in how students learn do not indicate an inability to learn or the need to categorize students according to learning disability labels. Rather, variations in students' learning often relate to different learning styles and prior knowledge. For example, students possess different backgrounds and prior knowledge that can affect their understanding of figurative language in a text passage. Unless teachers are able to use proximal instruction strategies to help each student comprehend the figurative language, some students' comprehension may be forever lacking.

Student differences in comprehension fluency, writing production, and information research effectiveness will become more visible to teachers working in networked classrooms. Teachers may notice that a student who has difficulty reading a grade-level trade book is able to read it with online links to **supportive text** that assists with comprehension. Another student may experience frustration reading aloud informational text due to vocabulary recall and language processing dysfunctions but comprehend the same informational text during silent reading at his own pace with access to an online multimedia dictionary. A third student may have difficulty concentrating her attention on audience questions during a verbal presentation but perform excellently when conducting an **asynchronous threaded discussion** about her **interactive multimedia** report published on the Internet.

In the study conducted by McNabb and colleagues (2002), teachers reported frequently using the Internet to accommodate students' diversity in a variety of ways. One teacher, for example, handed a notecard to each of her fourth-grade students and asked them to complete one of three activities listed on it. She designed all three activities to teach students how to use an online thesaurus. Without explicitly saying that the three assignments were at different levels, the teacher enabled each student to adapt the assignment to his or her own instructional level. Teachers also reported working one on one with students, assigning

supportive text:

Print enhanced with hyperlinks to text or interactive multimedia.

asynchronous threaded discussion:

An online forum for participants to communicate with a time delay.

interactive multimedia:

Related multimodal information that can be presented together with hyperlinks.

group projects in which students chose their roles, and designing open-ended assignments that allowed students to shape the criteria and methods for their literacy development. In order to use and understand these types of proximal instruction practices online, teachers need to understand the dynamics of digital reading and writing.

Understanding Dynamics of Digital Reading

Reading online tends to demand more comprehension monitoring than reading print. Reading for context online also is more challenging, especially during information research activities. Conversely, students who struggle with print may find the interactive multimedia options embedded in hypertext helpful for deriving meaning from words on the screen if taught how to access online texts for that purpose. While literacy researchers are just beginning to examine how the interactivity of digital texts changes reading (Kamil et al., 2000), it is clear that reading hypertext and interactive multimedia texts complicates becoming literate in **networked cultures** (Leu & Kinzer, 2000). Overall, the interactive nature of digital texts puts the locus of control in the hands of students on a much greater scale than static print.

networked culture:
A geographical community connected through Internet access to participants in the global village.

In the 1960s, a computer scientist named Theodor Nelson coined the term *hypertext* to describe digital texts (Landow, 1992). Reading hypertext is a different experience than reading linear print (Bolter, 1992, 1998; Landow, 1992; Rouet, Levonen, Dillon, & Spiro, 1996). Print materials tend to be arranged in a hierarchy of ideas with established text structures. Narrative literature, for example, typically is organized around a plot, characters, and specific settings with a chronological order of incidents and episodes that convey a specific message. Informational texts may use a variety of text structures such as compare-and-contrast, persuasive argument, or problem–solution narratives. Historical and biographical accounts also have commonly used text structures. Fluent readers acquire knowledge of text structures and store that knowledge in long-term memory for later retrieval during reading. Prior knowledge of text structures supports the development of readers' comprehension fluency. In contrast, hypertext is characterized by chunks of information that are linked together **multisequentially** or without the use of conventional text structures, which challenges readers to create their own narrative sequence while making selective reading choices. Landow (1992) points out the dilemma many readers have with hypertexts as a result:

multisequential:
Allows for diverse reading options in a single hypertext.

lexia:
A single block of narrative, images, sounds, or other media within a hypertext.

> Electronic links connect **lexias** "external" to a work—say, commentary on it by another author or parallel or contrasting texts—as well as within it and thereby create text that is experienced as nonlinear, or, more properly, as multilinear or multisequential. Although conventional reading habits apply within each lexia, once one leaves the shadowy bounds of any text unit or node, new rules and new experience apply. (p. 4)

Landow explains that traditional reading conventions and strategies only apply within a single lexia of hypertext on a screen. When readers click on a **hyperlink**, they are transported to another lexia, which may entail a different context on the Web. The association of one lexia of information on the Web to another is not always explicit or even logical. The hyperlinks that connect one author's text to another's text may be the work of a third party altogether. As a result, reading hypertext involves making many more decisions, based on prior knowledge or a reader's predictions, than does a cohesive printed text.

Cognitive Demands of Reading Hypertext. Because of its multisequential nature, hypertext requires that readers apply heightened comprehension-monitoring skills for meaning making. Comprehension monitoring is a metacognitive skill that enables good readers to maintain awareness of meaning and to regulate their ability to attain meaning from a text as a whole during the act of reading (Harris & Hodges, 1995). For students with effective language processing, comprehension monitoring is nearly automatic (Levine, 2002). When students monitor their comprehension of a text, they are keenly aware of when they do or do not understand the meaning of words in relationship to each other. In contrast, students with poor comprehension monitoring are not aware that they do not understand the meaning of a text. Established print-based text structures help authors to explain their meanings to readers. In online environments, the demand for comprehension monitoring increases because of the unclear associations between hypertext lexia and the disruption of familiar text structures.

Knowledge of print-based text structures relieves the cognitive load for attention and memory when reading (Aebersold & Field, 1997), while reading hypertext can easily overload the limited capacity of active working memory (Walz, 2001). *Working memory* is a technical term that refers to the active portion of long-term memory that determines the recall of vocabulary and prior knowledge about word meanings, text structures, and context (Baddeley, Logie, Nimmo-Smith, & Brereton, 1985; Just & Carpenter, 1992; Wenger & Payne, 1996). Active working memory "serves as a temporary way station, a place where ideas are stored while they are being developed further, manipulated, or used as part of an activity" (Levine, 2002, p. 75). Heller (1990) reviewed early studies about the use of hypertext and interactive multimedia in education and uncovered problems of disorientation, cognitive overload, lack of commitment, and aimless surfing among readers of clickable digital texts. An overloaded working memory interrupts the fluency with which a student comprehends. As a result, comprehending hypertext can be a daunting task for struggling readers who lack adequate working memory to hold in their immediate consciousness what they have read.

Navigating through hypertext is a cognitive process simultaneously calling for reading (i.e., comprehension strategies) and writing (i.e., authoring choices).

keyword search:
A query composed
of carefully selected
words on a research
topic.

Because hypertexts typically contain many reading options and interactive multimedia text formats, a reader may be able to adapt the text to his or her own level by conducting **keyword searches** or clicking on supportive text linked to and from particular webpages. However, these are comprehension-monitoring strategies that require prior knowledge of hypertext structures and strong attention and memory capacity. When teachers observe students in a networked classroom, students may look more engaged than when using print materials, but that does not necessarily mean their comprehension follows. In networked classrooms, it is imperative for teachers to observe and monitor how well students comprehend the texts they interact with online.

Hypertext exponentially expands the avenues for exploration and learning while it requires readers to make inferences and draw associations between lexias. Readers with well-developed comprehension-monitoring skills are compelled to compare and contrast author perspectives and the credibility of the evidence they present. Online, readers need to have a purpose that steers their reading decisions. They also need to acquire the habits of mind for synthesizing and corroborating information across information sources. In addition, they need to be flexible in exploring new avenues of thought and persistent in relating new ideas to their prior knowledge. The cognitive demands of previewing, scanning, and clicking through volumes of hypertexts can be overwhelming or highly engaging, depending on the reader's ability to create a cohesive narrative while focusing on a purposeful search for meaning. In contrast, print readers follow the inherent structure of the text, which is purposefully narrated by the author for a specific audience, but online readers have to create their own narration as they actively click from one lexia to the next.

Students who do not actively monitor their comprehension may develop disjointed narratives in their working memory, which can be mentally exhausting or incomprehensible. Variance among students' attention and memory spans may cause some to become frustrated or disinterested during online reading activities. Students who lack strong metacognitive-monitoring abilities will most likely experience disorientation when reading hypertext. The hypertext and interactive multimedia found on the World Wide Web, in particular, are not explicitly designed for instructional use at a particular reading level. As a result, young adolescents who are still developing their metacognitive-monitoring strategies for comprehension fluency and critical reading can easily experience disorientation online. In this context, disorientation refers to the act of getting lost online so as not to know where you are or how to return to some starting point (Lockard & Abrams, 2004). In addition to disorientation, students with weak comprehension-monitoring skills or deficits in working memory and attention may also experience cognitive overload, an overwhelming feeling that will hinder their ability to cope with the many lexia options online or to synthesize the lexias they read in a meaningful way. When this occurs, teachers who are actively monitoring students' online reading processes can intervene with proximal instruction strategies to scaffold students' comprehension. Effective interactive curricula are carefully designed to provide a cohesive collection of hypertext and interactive multimedia, or supportive text, options that reduce the cognitive load for struggling readers.

Anderson-Inman and Horney (1998) coined the term *supportive text*, which refers to readings enhanced with hyperlinks to related lexia that elaborate, define, or explain content. When purposefully designed to alleviate cognitive overload, supportive text can help improve readers' comprehension. Anderson-Inman and Horney (1998) and McKenna (1998) strategically selected digital materials to link keywords or concepts to more print, sound, or graphics that further explained or elaborated on the central meaning of a print lexia. The purpose of supportive text is to scaffold students' reading at various reading levels. Designing online curriculum resources as supportive texts ensures that all students, whose reading abilities differ, will improve their comprehension within a particular lesson or unit. Students also come to literacy learning activities with varying perspectives, prior knowledge, and interests that can be addressed within a supportive text. When designed appropriately to address the variance among a particular group of students, the interactive curriculum can enhance rather than deter students' reading development.

Cognitive Demands of Online Research. In order for students to be successful researchers, they have to apply critical reading skills efficiently to locate and evaluate information suitable to their research purpose within a given time frame. The process of identifying online information relevant to a research topic is often complicated by the seemingly infinite hypertext lexias available and variance in author credibility. Although there are benefits to using the Internet for research purposes, there also are aspects of hypertexts that may cause some students to have difficulty remembering what they access on the screen. For example, Internet **search engines** may pull together unrelated information in a **search return list** that looks like a table of contents, but it does not serve the same function. The hypertext structure of a search result list often displays texts by unrelated authors. In addition, if the keywords used in the search query include words that have multiple definitions, the topics listed may range widely.

Konishi (2003) reports research about the metacognitive comprehension-monitoring strategies used by skilled readers conducting information research on the World Wide Web. Findings indicate that the participating students set goals for skimming, searching, and scanning online texts. They also routinely employed navigation strategies such as backtracking or retracing their **hypertext link path**, using search engines to locate information, scrolling, browsing available links, and opening a new browser window. These are some of the strategies emerging

search engine:
An online program used to index and access contents of registered websites.

search return list:
A collection of Web resources compiled by a search engine.

hypertext link path:
A reader's clickable text sequence through hypertext or interactive multimedia.

to deal with the hundreds of hypertext reading options and shifting contents within a given website that online researchers encounter.

Conducting online research requires skill at detecting changes in context when linking from one lexia of hypertext to another. Hypertext readers can start out at a credible website and quickly stumble onto questionable sites. Cues such as changes in authorship, purpose, lexicon, and host **domain** signal a shift in context. Teachers can demonstrate for students how following links within a website may help readers understand the meaning of a word or shift their reading context to another topic altogether. When researching online, students will encounter multisequential links to and from different authors, cultures, and organizations that may have no other affiliation than through a hypertext link. Rouet and colleagues (1996) explain that, in hypertext, "Semantic relations between units are not always explicitly represented...hypertext readers may make incoherent transitions between hypertext units" (p. 19). Navigating through various websites requires that students read critically and transfer their understanding of context from one website to another because the quality of connective links in hypertext is not easily controlled online.

Students in the middle grades typically approach online information gathering in a rushed fashion, however, rather than taking the time for critical reading. They may not stop to read at all. Williams (2004) explains,

> Beyond decoding words and sentences, we think of a reader as a person who makes particular kinds of intertextual connections, who asks particular kinds of questions of a text, who reads at a particular intellectual distance from the text, who talks about more than the text's meaning and analyzes its nature. (¶ 7)

Teachers who use proximal instruction intervene to scaffold students' critical reading, which is essential to comprehending hypertext while conducting information research. Some students whose attention spans are short or whose mental energy is weak will need extra prodding to help them focus on critical reading during information-gathering activities. Chunking research opportunities into a series of incremental information search and evaluation tasks can provide students with structured reading experiences that lead to successful comprehension of informational hypertexts. Critical reading during information research is especially taxing because it requires students to be fluent in comprehending the multiple and potentially disparate contexts in which hypertext links or search engine return lists situate information on the screen. Comprehension monitoring and active working memory also are needed to sort out credible author perspectives from multiple sources.

When conducting think-aloud sessions with students who were researching online, I discovered that they like to look at cues such as visual displays and the amount of advertising on the screen. One student explained it to me this way:

domain:
The Web address for an organizational or personal website.

Webpages that look appealing must be credible because it takes a lot of money and manpower to support nice graphics. This logic, however, is not accurate, as demonstrated by the hoax website lesson in chapter 4; hoax and commercially biased websites that present unreliable information to unsuspecting readers may be just as visually appealing as more credible Web resources.

Young adolescent students growing up in networked cultures expect immediate answers to their questions. Many who have little instruction about researching on the Internet become adept at locating information on the Internet—or so they think. Because of the instant response to their search queries, their attention span can be reduced. If they do not find information they want within a few seconds, they move on to a new site. They find answers on the Internet, although the answers may not be credible. Left on their own, they acquire search skills that limit their research results. They often do not see the need to go through an in-depth process to locate information online. Because there are so many distractions and reading options, students with attention problems may be distracted easily or unable to focus long enough to create meaning from the hypertexts they read. Much reading online is actually information research, which requires a persistent focus on a reading objective. To avoid aimlessly surfing, each student must stay alert while making reading choices. Teachers can address weaknesses in students' memory or attention by providing them with appropriate online assignment options aligned with their personal reading goals and interests.

Understanding Dynamics of Digital Writing

Like differences in students' reading processes, differences in the development of students' writing processes tend to be latent or not observable in classrooms in which teachers do not interact directly with students as they write. When using a writing curriculum that only focuses on assessing writing products, it is nearly impossible to understand the causes of students' learning problems related to writing. The networked classroom, however, is different; there teachers have more opportunities to interact with students as they actually write. Proximal instruction enables teachers to interact with students during the writing process and provides teachers with opportunities to observe variance in students' cognitive processes that affect their ability to develop as writers. Differences in students' metacognitive monitoring, attention span, memory capacity, or spatial processing may manifest as differences in students' writing output. These are functional aspects of the brain that help students organize their written language production (Levine, 2002; Schunk, 1991).

Educators' current understandings of written language production processes derive from research that shifted writing instruction methods away from a focus on written products to a focus on the process of writing. During the 1980s, researchers identified stages of the writing process, including brainstorming to generate ideas, drafting to organize ideas, monitoring writing production, and revising to focus ideas into a coherent narrative (Flower & Hayes, 1980; Scardamalia & Bereiter, 1986). Flower and Hayes, in particular, emphasized the important role of metacognitive monitoring during production of written language. Monitoring occurs to steer revisions that connect semantics and syntax in a logical flow of ideas to convey the writer's purpose.

The writing process is one of the most complex academic tasks a student encounters. Generating initial ideas during brainstorming and organizing ideas from a brainstorming session into a coherent writing purpose are a challenge for most middle-level students. As shown in chapter 5, these skills relate to producing the macrostructure for a text. Applying correct spelling, grammar, punctuation, sentence syntax, or vocabulary choices relates to production of the microstructure of a text. In addition, students are often learning to apply story or text structures and to express their personal viewpoints still under development in the middle grades. Their opinions, beliefs, values, and expressive abilities may shift as they begin to understand themselves as writers. Students' text production may break down anywhere in the complex writing process.

Cognitive Demands of Audience Awareness. Students may exhibit significant differences in their awareness of social context and audience, which may impede their ability to reflect upon and monitor their own writing process. A writer's awareness of audience and of the social context for writing often shapes how he or she conveys a message. One way for students to develop awareness of their audience's interests, prior knowledge, and cultural biases toward a topic is through scaffolded interactions with members of the target audience. Research indicates students are more motivated to monitor and revise their writing when they write for publication to a real audience or learning community on the Internet (Brandjes, 1997; Wood, 2000).

When planning to host online audience events with young adolescent writers, it is important to carefully craft and train audience participants to use proximal instruction strategies to engage individual students in reader response interactions. Audience members can be invited to read and respond to students' **blogs** in a structured manner, for example. Methods for organizing online interactions among students and external partners are described in more detail in chapter 6. Supportive adults can be enlisted to participate as online audience members to respond to students' work using question prompts and writing rubrics provided by teachers to scaffold students' reflection and metacognitive-monitoring habits, particularly in the revision stage of writing. Although "revision is a difficult skill for students to acquire, and it constitutes one of the stumbling blocks of writing instruction" (Joram, Woodruff, Bryson, & Lindsay, 1992, p. 169), requiring students to act upon feedback from audience members about a work in progress needs to be timely.

blog:
A Web log with dated entries that functions as an online journal.

Most middle-level students have a strong need for belonging and approval that can lead them to overreact to feedback they perceive as embarrassing or ridiculing (NMSA, 2003b). This tendency is aggravated by changes in self-identity spurred on by the growth and development cycles of young adolescence. Teachers need to assess individual students' readiness for reader response and audience interaction activities. If a student does not possess strong confidence in his or her ability for self-expression and personal insights, the student may not respond positively to audience feedback despite its objective value. Students who are typically perceived as unpopular within a peer group or exhibit social inability need extra support forming a trusting bond with an online writing mentor. Teachers can pair these students with audience participants who are known to have the emotional intelligence to respond to students' writing in ways that accommodate those with low self-efficacy. When structured to address developmental diversity, online writer–audience interaction can help students hone their writing skills as well as metacognitive-monitoring abilities that are transferable to other literacy activities in the global village.

Cognitive Demands of Online Dialogue. In networked classrooms, some students who engage in online dialogue may actually increase their fluency with written language production. Despite the potential benefits of interacting online with writing mentors and audience members during the writing process, students with written language production dysfunctions may be easily overwhelmed in the fast-paced networked classroom. Spatial-processing problems, for example, can disrupt the flow of the writing production process. Students with weak spatial-processing abilities have difficulty making associations between letters, a picture or diagram, and visual interpretation in the mind's eye (Levine, 2002). For students with weak spatial abilities, generating letters and words does not come automatically. Online, written language production also requires students to exert enormous amounts of focused attention and to activate their working memory. Writers need a strong active working memory to help them recall knowledge of grammar, vocabulary, and concepts during the act of writing.

Students with attention, memory, or spatial-processing dysfunctions may engage happily in face-to-face discussions but hesitate to communicate during synchronous chats. In addition, students who struggle with written language production may need additional support during synchronous writing sessions to generate and post their ideas. Observant teachers may notice these students are able to produce writing when given more time to reflect and to access memory or attention aids but cannot keep up with the rapid read–write cycles inherent in synchronous chats. For these students, the asynchronous discussion mode is a viable option that allows them to participate in online dialogue but alleviates the time pressures for writing and reading posted messages from other participants.

Synchronous chats generate visually incoherent strings of texts (see chat transcripts in chapter 5, for example; however, those excerpts were edited to highlight segments of the chats most pertinent to the purpose of the chapter). The visual disorganization of chats is the result of a time lag from when a participant posts his or her comment in reference to others' posted comments. The faster a participant can produce and post his comment, the closer it appears in the chat window to the comment to which it refers. The fast flow of postings can be controlled somewhat by the number of participants involved. The more participants, the more a student has to read through the chat transcript to identify comments to which he or she wants to respond.

To complicate matters, several different topics of discussion often emerge among participants in a chat. Synchronous chats require intense attention to read and respond quickly. Those who effortlessly engage in synchronous chat or instant messaging modes of online communications typically possess fluent writing skills. These modes of communication resemble brief conversations that happen in person (Wallace, 1999). The sessions can easily become streams of consciousness among young adolescents, which may be a benefit if the instructional purpose is to stimulate creative thinking or brainstorm new ideas among a group of young writers.

chat acronym:
Slang used in online dialogue to save keystrokes.

Because of the value of short response times, participants of synchronous chats typically do not stop to use a spell checker or to check their syntax. Students make many spelling errors and often use abbreviated word symbols or **chat acronyms** that complicate word recognition. Their main objective is getting their message posted before the conversation meanders. This can be disorienting and unproductive for students with poor spatial-processing abilities.

Online chats also require strong comprehension monitoring and attention span. Students need to juggle their understanding of the social context for writing with their procedural and informational knowledge held in active working memory. They need to be able to comprehend quickly the context to which a posted comment refers. They may need to scroll and search for the context if they lose attention. They need to be simultaneous readers and writers as well as good at computer keyboarding.

In networked classrooms, synchronous chats may be most useful for peer-to-peer sharing or one-on-one tutoring sessions with individual students. Teachers can set up pair-sharing chats among students and then electronically visit their discussions to provide instructional guidance and feedback in relation to the discussion assignment. Online dialogue sessions have the benefit of generating a record of students' submitted drafts or chat transcripts. Teachers can review these archives to assess difficulties students may have orchestrating the many tasks involved in producing a polished text.

Distributive Communities Online

The notion of distributive communities with relation to learning is well grounded in research spanning many decades. In communities with strong cultural ties, adults tend to mediate learning experiences using strategies like those discussed in the previous section. Mediating students' learning is vital to cognitive development and functions of the brain that allow learning to occur (Boyer, 1995; Dewey, 1990; Vygotsky, 1934/1978). Years of research conducted by Feuerstein, Klein, and Tannenbaum (1991) verify children's inherent need for cultural continuity to aid their cognitive development and learning to learn abilities. In a study conducted by Williams and Sternberg (1988), findings indicate that a group of individuals engaged in isolated learning events may not achieve at the same rate of progress as they would if they were engaged in social learning events. Williams and Sternberg measured social effectiveness and found it to be a better predictor of group performance than the group members' individual IQ test scores. These results suggest that an effective group enables its individual members to excel more in their learning progress than they would be able to do through isolated learning experiences.

For middle-level students, who typically are grappling with their sense of identity and autonomy, strong learning communities play a fundamental role in school achievement (NMSA, 2003b). Experts explain that middle-level students may search for adult acceptance, especially from parents, but also are very concerned about fitting in with peers (NMSA, 2003b). They often experiment with new behaviors as they search for a social identity. They also like recognition for their efforts and often overreact to ridicule, embarrassment, and rejection and, thus, are socially vulnerable. It makes sense, then, to spend time and effort to arrange for community-based learning activities at the middle level. The challenge has to do with creating a social culture conducive to learning in the intangible, text-based environment online.

Establishing Community Rules of Engagement

Groups in networked cultures have opportunities to form, adapt, and dissolve much more rapidly and fluidly than in geographical time and space. Online groups often bypass traditional group norming and conformity pressures. To counteract this phenomenon, a form of etiquette unique to online environments—**netiquette**—has evolved. Those familiar with online interaction take it seriously. Shea (2004a), a well-known netiquette author, explains,

netiquette:
Online communication etiquette.

> Simply stated, it's network etiquette—that is, the etiquette of cyberspace. And "etiquette" means "the forms required by good breeding or prescribed by authority to be required in social or official life." In other words, Netiquette is a set of rules for behaving properly online.

When you enter any new culture—and cyberspace has its own culture—you're liable to commit a few social blunders. You might offend people without meaning to. Or you might misunderstand what others say and take offense when it's not intended. To make matters worse, something about cyberspace makes it easy to forget that you're interacting with other real people—not just ASCII characters on a screen, but live human characters. (¶ 2)

Shea (2004b) later adds,

And because Netiquette is different in different places, it's important to know where you are. Thus the next corollary:

Lurk before you leap

When you enter a domain of cyberspace that's new to you, take a look around. Spend a while listening to the chat or reading the archives. Get a sense of how the people who are already there act. Then go ahead and participate. (¶ 4)

lurk:
To read messages in a chat room or online forum without participating.

Teachers who are planning to initiate online literature circles, for example, can ease into managing discussions by establishing the netiquette, or rules of engagement, for students. Making the rules explicit and reinforcing them during online events are important aspects of managing group interactions in a noninvasive manner. Rules set the boundaries for students and help establish norms for the distributive learning community to emerge and flourish. A fundamental rule for online groups pertains to participation among all members of the learning community. Teachers are wise to include a no lurking rule in their netiquette to help ensure participation from all students.

As mentioned earlier in this chapter, an indicator of a successful learning community is distributive participation. Many traditional, teacher-led classrooms are dominated by interactions between the teacher and a few students. In thriving learning communities, however, adults and students step in and out of the teaching role—that is, everyone contributes to the group's learning. A student may need extra encouragement to move from the role of spectator to one who fully participates. In distributive learning communities, teachers may take the lead by modeling participation techniques, explaining content, and facilitating dialogue.

Researchers who have studied patterns of computer-mediated communication explain that they fundamentally differ from face-to-face communication patterns (Cognition and Technology Group at Vanderbilt, 1997; Riel & Harasim, 1994; Wallace, 1999). Teachers tend to lose control of online communications, and control of dialogue patterns becomes more distributive among the group's members. Students who are reluctant to participate in face-to-face discussions may find a voice online. Students who are overly ambitious and dominate face-to-face discussions may find their peers challenging their ideas for the first time. And as student behaviors shift, netiquette and rules of engagement can help foster trust and respect among those in an online group.

Facilitating Community Trust Building

Trust building is another aspect of community that requires extra attention online. Students engaged in **online literacy learning** may not have any prior knowledge of one another, or they may have experienced negative interactions during face-to-face activities. As a result, they may be reluctant to engage in meaningful online dialogue that exposes their lack of knowledge, questions, new ideas, or critical thinking about a topic at hand. And because dialogue online is written, it is more visible and permanent than verbal dialogue. It generates a tangible archive of students' learning progress but at the same time exposes students' vulnerabilities in written form for all to see. Although online dialogue is more permanent than verbal dialogue, students do have the option to revise their thinking as they generate comments during online discussions. This is best done before posting a comment to the group. Simply refraining from clicking the "submit" or "send" button also is an option online. As a result, students tend to be more reflective and cognizant of the social context to which they are contributing during online events, which can lead to trustworthy learning communities.

In a face-to-face context, there are nonverbal cues that set the tone for trust building; however, online, the text alone holds the cues. Wallace (1999) analyzes the psychological aspect of online interactions and dialogue and explains that without the benefit of nonverbal cues, friendly disagreements can be perceived as verbal aggression. These types of online **posts** invite **flame wars** involving character attacks, foul language, and argumentative statements. One way online communicators have addressed this problem is with the sincere use of **emoticons**, which have been successful in reducing misperceptions that lead to flaming. Teachers also can use icebreaker activities to introduce members of a distributive community to each other online and follow up with periodic online social activities that can help students establish and maintain group affiliations (Finders, 1997). Online learning communities that are well organized and supportive play a positive role in students' identity formation and ownership of literacy. Teachers play an important role by modeling interactions online that convey to students it is safe to explore new ideas and question others' understanding of content.

McNabb (2001) lists the following techniques emerging from online communities that foster mutual trust and a sense of belonging:

- engaging in a team-building exercise as a beginning online group activity;
- posting personal profiles within the group workspace to share backgrounds, interests, and aspirations related to the group tasks and goals;
- interacting in assigned peer-sharing tasks with clear roles and responsibilities for individual and team follow through;
- establishing timelines for assigned interactions and task completion activities and reinforcing published consequences for untimely or freeloading behaviors;

online literacy learning:
Reading, writing, and information research activities that occur via the Internet.

post:
A message submitted during online dialogue.

flame war:
A sequence of hostile messages exchanged online.

emoticon:
A group of keyboard characters used to express emotion.

- modeling risk-taking, respect for participant contributions, and tolerance for multiple-perspective sharing and learning differences. (¶ 14)

These are some of the strategies that enable teachers to build trust among students in online groups. Actions to reduce anonymity and establish real-world consequences for online behaviors, both positive and negative, motivate students to take responsibility for their contributions. Teachers can use instant messaging, for example, to privately prompt students whose participation is waning or whose behavior violates established netiquette and rules of engagement. In the online environment in which students are collectively interacting, it is easier for teachers to review participation rates among students and to address individual problems without interrupting the entire group.

Fostering Peer Collaboration

The literacy researchers interviewed in the study conducted by McNabb and colleagues (2002) emphasized the value of online collaboration for fostering literacy development among students. They encouraged teachers to allow their students to build online relationships with other student groups in order to engage in joint projects, gather information otherwise inaccessible, or share their reactions to a common reading. They suggested that it is especially valuable for students to communicate with their peers in other locations. They explained that the Internet should not be viewed as a packaged curriculum for teaching literacy but rather as a social environment in which students can pose and answer genuine questions related to reading and writing assignments. One participating researcher defined effective Internet-using teachers as those who can develop highly social environments for their students.

Shields and Behrman (2000) report on a series of research studies that document the need for Internet-based learning opportunities to do a better job of fostering healthy community-building strategies among school-age children. In the middle grades, students are developing personal value systems and becoming concerned with major societal issues. They need opportunities for positive interactions with adults who will take them seriously and scaffold their becoming responsible citizens (NMSA, 2003b). Online, myriad cultures merge, which adds to students' interest in spontaneous or informal **threads** on current events or social philosophies, and they may spend hours engaged in these types of online literacy activities after school. Their time online is not always conducive to their overall well-being, however. Shields and Behrman (2000) also report a possible link between increases in teenage loneliness and depression and the amount of time teens spend in synchronous chats, randomly interacting with strangers who have no stake in their development. They recommend that online social ties support and facilitate strong, nurturing interpersonal relationships for students to com-

thread:
A running log of asynchronous posts on the same topic.

bat these issues. Kraut and colleagues (1998) report on the positive benefits of strong community-based uses of the Internet that allow students to spend time interacting in nurturing relationships with friends, peers, family, teachers, mentors, and caring professionals. Rules of engagement, trust building, and clear collaboration roles help foster positive experiences online.

In the case of cross-cultural learning communities, my experience suggests that the time for introducing these interactions is after students have positive online experiences with an established local community. Cross-cultural groups have inherent challenges pertaining to differences in language, time and space, or cultural context that can complicate online collaborations. Online groups that do not have a prior history tend to form quickly around projects, events, or ideas and can easily disperse. According to Wallace (1999),

> Despite the ephemeral and fragile nature of so many forums on the Internet there is evidence that a very strong sense of "groupness" does emerge regularly, though the magic that creates this in one group but not another is not entirely clear. (p. 56)

Groups that exist only online are more temporary than face-to-face groups who may have a history and future beyond the life of the online activity. Therefore, teachers who want to engage their students in cross-cultural learning communities are well served by collaborating with other online teachers to generate common rules of engagement and collaborative goals that provide unity for students and help counteract any tendency toward discontinuity in remote online groups.

Conclusion

The Internet is a shifting literacy landscape. It can appear to be a highly unorganized learning environment when compared with nonnetworked classrooms. Nonetheless, it provides valuable curriculum resources and communications networks that can support literacy development in ways otherwise unavailable to students. Attending to developmental differences among students can help create an effective literacy learning experience in networked classrooms. Although establishing a distributive learning community is a pedagogical challenge, proximal instruction assists teachers in adapting their instructional approach to respond to differences among students' reading and writing processes. At the same time, the learning community approach allows students to develop awareness of themselves as unique learners within social contexts that affect their literacy performance. Taking a proximal instruction approach within a distributive learning community enables students to eventually internalize strategies for self-monitoring their participation in online literacy acts. Chapter 3 illustrates how two teachers scaffold students' participation in online literature circles. The ways they organize the online learning activities allow them to adapt their instruction and curriculum design to address diversity among students' comprehension fluency and foster ownership of literacy.

GUIDING QUESTIONS FOR DISCUSSION

1. How similar or dissimilar is the description of pedagogy in this chapter to the pedagogy in your classroom?

2. What is your personal reaction to the notion of proximal instruction to facilitate a distributive learning community?

3. What benefits and potential difficulties do you perceive for literacy learning in networked classrooms?

4. What implications do the ideas in this chapter have for your own professional development needs with regard to managing diversity among students' online literacy activities?

CHAPTER 3

Fostering Ownership of Literacy Online

When I think about ownership of literacy, the face of a student I interviewed at an urban middle school comes to mind. I was visiting the school to evaluate its **wireless** laptop program when the student told me about his experience using the **Internet** during school hours. He said one of the things he liked most about having the laptop was that he could communicate with his father throughout the day using **instant messaging**—until one day when his teacher caught him typing on the keyboard during her presentation. The teacher told him that instant messaging was forbidden even if it was his father on the other end of the communications. I still remember the student's face as he looked at me with discouragement and confusion in his eyes and asked, "Why can't I tell my dad what we're doing in class?" Later, I learned that the student did not have permission under the school's Internet policy to communicate with anyone outside the classroom despite the technical capability to do so via the wireless network on campus. His teachers and administrators were leery of students connecting with others beyond the school walls, so they decided to adopt a policy forbidding it rather than finding ways to manage students' interactions in the **global village**.

School policies and practices that do not teach students appropriate use of online literacy tools make little sense. Likewise, ignoring the Internet does not make it go away. Digital reading and writing are the modes of choice for most students growing up in **networked cultures**. Tapscott (1998) found that 8- to 14-year-old U.S. youths spend up to two hours after school daily engaging in peer-to-peer online reading and writing conferences, **synchronous chat** groups, and other forms of telecommunications involving digital texts. Surprisingly, a recent study conducted by Nielsen (2005) indicates that adolescents are less successful than adults at completing online tasks applicable to literate citizenship. When researchers asked participants of the study to visit educational and health resources, news and entertainment, and e-commerce and nonprofit foundation websites, adolescents

wireless:
Transmission of information without cables or cords.

Internet:
Global Infrastructure of information and communication networks.

instant messaging:
One-on-one online dialogue in real time.

global village:
Networked cultures around the world connected via the Internet.

networked culture:
A geographical community connected through Internet access to participants in the global village.

synchronous chat:
Real-time exchange of online dialogue between multiple participants.

performed poorly due to insufficient reading and information research skills and less tolerance for websites they considered boring or difficult to figure out (Nielsen, 2005). These results indicate that while students may appear to be savvy Web users, they still need guidance to develop the literacy skills needed to make sense of the **hypertext** and **interactive multimedia** resources on the Web.

hypertext:
Digital print with hyperlinks readers click on to access other texts.

interactive multimedia:
Related multimodal information that can be presented together with hyperlinks.

Students growing up in the global village face increasing demands to acquire new knowledge through informational text. Online, students encounter more new vocabulary and a richer context for understanding facts, perspectives, or themes than in a textbook. The interactivity of texts and modes of dialogue online allows students to explore literacy learning on an individual basis and empowers them to find their voice and to follow text connections of personal interest. They also acquire a proclivity for learning and applying literacy skills to satisfy their curiosity about life. As a result, students who are motivated to read and write experience ownership of literacy. In networked cultures, Tapscott (1998) explains, youth create online communities of their own to pursue personal interests. They become adept at using online communication tools and teach each other the literacy norms, forms, and conventions of networked cultures. The Internet is the place where youth go to engage in literacy acts that are meaningful to their social life and to enrich their understanding of the world around them. They are intrinsically motivated to read and write online.

The Role of Motivation in Literacy Learning

Motivation, enjoyment, and engagement are key factors in advancing along a continuum of lifelong literacy development, according to recent research findings (e.g., Kamil, 2003; Sen, Partelow, & Miller, 2005). Young adolescents can acquire ownership of literacy by engaging in literacy learning events online that also facilitate their academic learning. According to Au (1997), ownership of literacy has as much to do with how one reads as it does with why one reads. The "how" includes literary aspects of literature content and form, language conventions, both social and text-based skills and strategies, and higher level thinking processes involved in comprehension and composition. The "why" ties in to reader motivation, background, and interests that are personal and diverse among students.

A primary approach for fostering students' ownership of literacy is to encourage reading and writing in areas of interest in order to help students develop comprehension of increasingly complex texts and to expose them to the pleasures of being literate. Students who are interested in reading are more likely to develop expertise in reading as well as in the content area they read. The importance of engaging students through their interests has been verified in cumulative research findings (APA Work Group of the Board of Educational Affairs, 1997; Alexander,

2003; Bransford et al., 1999). In her presidential address at the National Reading Conference, synthesizing years of research about language arts curricula, Kathryn Au states that "ownership of literacy needs to be the overarching goal of the curriculum. Ownership may be defined as students' valuing literacy" (p. 5). Au explains that students who value literacy have positive attitudes regarding it and freely engage in self-directed literacy activities at school and at home.

Experts claim that engaging students in daily reading activities that provide the appropriate amount of guidance helps foster their overall achievement in school (NICHD, 2000). To support students in the throes of their literacy development, Moore and colleagues (1999) recommend providing them with time to read, choice in reading materials, and facilitated events involving student-to-student and student-to-adult discourse about texts they read. This chapter highlights how two teachers use the Internet to provide these types of reading opportunities for students.

The interdisciplinary unit, titled Huck Finn's Journey, incorporates online literature circles and historical research in ways that deepen students' comprehension of the American classic *The Adventures of Huckleberry Finn* (Twain, 1884/2003) and its real-life historical context. (For resources and tips to learn more about literature circle methods, see the suggested websites in Table 1.) Teachers Balazs Dibuz and Drew Shilhanek foster their sixth-grade students' ownership of literacy by tapping into the dynamic power of the Internet to help scaffold their literary analysis of the historical novel and related informational texts.

TABLE 1
Literature Circle Web Resources

http://fac-staff.seattleu.edu/kschlnoe/web/LitCircles
The College of Education at Seattle University hosts an online Literature Circles Resource Center.

www.allamericareads.org/lessonplan/strategies/during/litcirc1.htm
The All America Reads project has compiled literature circle strategies and worksheets for teachers to use to help boost students' reading comprehension.

http://teacher.scholastic.com/professional/techexpert/litcircles3.htm
Technology in the classroom expert Julie Wood discusses how to take literature circles online.

Internet Tip: Website content and location shift periodically. Although care has been taken to list reliable websites, sometimes sponsors change or move webpages without notice to their readers. To find additional resources on literature circles, conduct a keyword search at www.google.com, or use your favorite search engine.

Keywords to Consider: *literature circle +online*

FIGURE 2
Characteristics of Learning Opportunities in the Huck Finn's Journey Unit

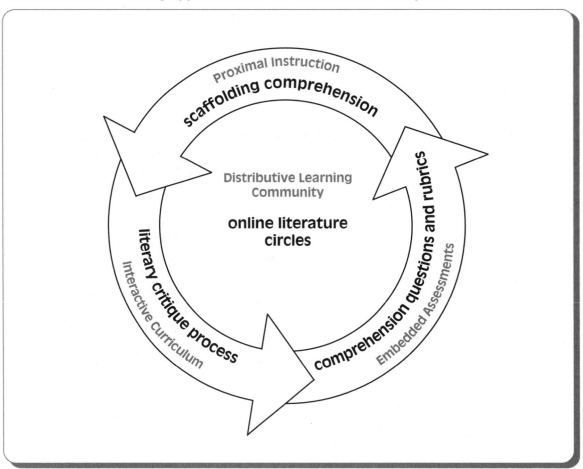

Figure 2 identifies the unit's features aligned with the framework for organizing **networked classrooms** using proximal instruction, interactive curriculum that fosters ownership of literacy, and embedded assessments that provide formative feedback for individual students within a distributive community of literacy learners, as discussed in chapter 1. The unit is a hybrid approach to using the Internet—some of the curricular activities occur without use of the Internet in the classroom and some occur online. Balazs and Drew used scaffolding strategies like those discussed in chapter 2 to guide students' deep comprehension of the novel and informational text they researched online.

networked classroom:
Environment in which students and teachers use the Internet for educational purposes.

Huck Finn's Journey

Curriculum Objective: To scaffold students' comprehension and critical reading of literature and related historical texts through online literature circles.

Materials: *The Adventures of Huckleberry Finn* (Twain, 1884/2003); daily access to online literature circles and historical websites via a password-protected **collaborative learning environment**.

Time Frame: Five weeks

Technology Standards: Addresses the NETS-S (ISTE, 1999) under the categories technology productivity tools, technology communications tools, and technology research tools.

Design of the Interactive Curriculum

Huck Finn's Journey is an interdisciplinary unit in which sixth-grade students study the period of Reconstruction in U.S. history while reading *The Adventures of Huckleberry Finn*. The unit merges reading the novel with reading informational text found through research about the time period of the characters in the book. When students began reading *Huckleberry Finn*, they already had read about Reconstruction in history textbooks, discussed the main issues of the era, and analyzed primary source documents online. They also role-played people and events from the Civil War to understand how people felt about the rebuilding of the United States in the late 1800s. Balazs and Drew then gave the students an overview of the setting of the novel, both geographically and historically. They encouraged students to pay attention to certain historical themes and issues in the novel. Balazs and Drew began the unit because they realized Huckleberry Finn's journey down the Mississippi offered opportunities for their sixth graders to explore the geography and society of that historical period, which positively affected their comprehension of the novel. Students were allowed to choose a topic and sources of informational text online in order to meet their historical research requirement. They learned to identify and apply literary elements and techniques authors use to convey meaning. They also honed their writing and information research skills and uses of technology to support their learning during this unit.

The teachers had been using the **World Wide Web** for research for about five years and often found open-ended Internet research activities frustrating for students and themselves. When they started using the Collaboratory (see www.collaboratory.nunet.net), a collaborative learning environment sponsored by Northwestern University for K–12 schools, they found the online research process was far more predictable and less time-consuming than they originally anticipated. Using an online service such as the Collaboratory provided teachers and students with access to a **cybrary**, in which teacher-selected websites are grouped

collaborative learning environment:
A password-protected workspace for groups.

World Wide Web:
Public portion of the Internet's online information resources.

cybrary:
An online library of World Wide Web resources.

by category and directly linked to the students' collaborative learning environment. Thus, online information resources are packaged with the assignment description online. In addition, students easily could engage in modes of online dialogue with teachers and fellow students within their online community to share ideas or ask for clarification about assignments. The cybrary for this unit included the website bibliography in Table 2. With teacher supervision and approval, students also were given time to conduct their own online searches for information they personally found relevant and interesting in the story's historical context. The basic assignment design required focusing on a teacher prompt, finding information to address the teachers' question about the places the characters visit or pass on their voyage down the Mississippi, and sharing research findings in the online literature circles.

During the five-week unit, the 32 students and two teachers met daily. Students read *Huckleberry Finn* in sections of approximately four chapters and answered questions while participating in literature discussions. Students were grouped with their peers into small literacy communities. Each group met face to face in the classroom and had the option of conducting online literature circles through the Collaboratory. The groups produced route maps that reflected their collective understanding of the novel and the period of history in which it is set. Although reading the novel and completing historical research can be accomplished within three weeks, the teachers intersperse the unit with language skills instruction. The skills instruction they provide involves grammar, vocabulary

TABLE 2
Web Resources for Huck Finn's Journey Research

www.digitalhistory.uh.edu/reconstruction/index.html
The University of Houston's website covers the social and economic conditions during Reconstruction with good primary source documents as well as scholarly, yet easily comprehended, information about this period in U.S. history.

www.davidestrada.com/river/extras/rivermap.html
David Estrada's account of his year of work and life on a Mississippi barge includes a simple map of the Mississippi River and its surrounding states, giving students a clear picture of the geography of the region and a useful tool for constructing their own route maps.

www.mississippiriverinfo.com
The Mississippi River Parkway Commission offers detailed information, including geographical and historical data, on the many communities along the Mississippi River.

http://search.eb.com/Blackhistory/article.do?nKeyValue=62908
Encyclopædia Britannica has a valuable source for studying the Reconstruction Period in U.S. history.

building, and daily oral language components. This approach spreads the unit throughout a five-week period according to the schedule in Table 3.

Through his teaching experience, Balazs has observed that sixth graders need prodding and sometimes direct instruction in literary analysis techniques to get the full meaning of the literature. They need to grow accustomed to idiomatic dialogue, for example. The story of *Huckleberry Finn* has plenty. It is not enough to grasp what is happening in the novel and what the characters feel or how they evolve. Students' comprehension is enhanced by learning to associate the events and attitudes in the novel with the historical context in which it was written and first released. For example, they learn to recognize and interpret Biblical and historical allusions. In order to fully appreciate the significance of a work such as *Huckleberry Finn*, students also must examine their own attitudes about race, friendship, truth, and the tension between individual beliefs and social mores. They learn to identify the effects of prejudice in the world around them. The historical literature also provides a means for students to discuss the realism of the writing and tie it to the period of Reconstruction and Reform in U.S. history. These comprehension strategies scaffold students' ownership of literacy.

TABLE 3
Huck Finn's Journey Activities and Assignments

Sequence	Events
Prerequisite	Students read about the American Reconstruction Era in history textbooks, discuss the main issues of that era, and analyze primary source documents online.
Ongoing	Students are assigned four-chapter sections to read daily during the course of the unit.
Days 1–11	Teacher introduces major section themes in the novel and explains historical background and relevant literary terms (e.g., irony, plot elements, character development techniques). Students form literature circles for face-to-face classroom discussions.
Day 12	Teachers pilot moving the literature circles online via an after-school session for interested students.
Days 13–17	Student participation in asynchronous threaded discussions becomes more elaborate and in depth as students start to lead their own discussion topics with teacher guidance.
Days 18–19	Student pairs conduct online information research to gather information about historical sites along the river to include on their route maps.
Days 20–23	Student groups create a route map, including paragraph-long descriptions of both historical and literary episodes along the route.
Days 24–25	Based on teacher feedback using the Route Map Rubric, students revise their route maps and complete comprehension test.

Organizing the Distributive Learning Community

The teachers first discovered the benefits of online literature circles when they began hosting **asynchronous threaded discussions** with students to scaffold their comprehension about books they were reading independently. In these online discussions, students were required monthly to choose a book from a list and produce a set of reading journal entries or a book review or participate in an online discussion about the book with a few of their peers. Balazs and Drew decided to continue using asynchronous threaded discussions to facilitate student discussion of the novel *Huckleberry Finn* because many students enjoyed exchanging ideas online. Students began by answering questions about *Huckleberry Finn* in small, face-to-face literature circles and then were invited to log on and respond to questions online. Students initially were given the option of participating in either the online or face-to-face literature circles. Those with greater comfort level and interest modeled for their peers how to participate in online dialogue. Eventually, the teachers required all students to participate in at least three rounds of online literature circles later in the unit.

After the teachers ascertained that enough students had successfully located the forum and could continue using this venue for their literature circle discussions, several class sessions were devoted to familiarizing more hesitant students with what their peers were doing online. The discussion momentum online grew from there. Eventually, the teachers selected more substantive themes from face-to-face discussions as prompts for students to elaborate and expand their thinking in the online discussions. This process resulted in students exploring the topics in greater depth and eventually posing their own questions and interpretations online.

In the face-to-face learning environment, there had been little time and few resources for students to share their private journal entries or book reviews. Online, student reflections could be shared more readily because of the time-delayed nature of the discussions. Students were provided Internet access during reading time in the networked classroom and could engage in online discussions as homework after school. Balazs observed that, online, the students tended to respond to one another's thinking with more substantial comments or probing questions, which resulted in higher levels of group comprehension than face-to-face discussions. Such an approach helped teach students critical reading techniques before hosting their discussions online.

Although the students engaged in higher order thinking online, Balazs also noticed that they had a tendency to use slang and simplified spellings, and omit punctuation. They felt comfortable playing with fun features of online **chat acronyms**, **emoticons**, and creative signatures. In response to these issues, the teachers established a general **netiquette** to remind students that proper grammar and mechanics were required in the asynchronous literature circle discussions because students had the opportunity to edit their writing before posting it. In contrast to the reflec-

asynchronous threaded discussion:
An online forum for participants to communicate with a time delay.

chat acronym:
Slang used in online dialogue to save keystrokes.

emoticon:
A group of keyboard characters used to express emotion.

netiquette:
Online communication etiquette.

tive nature of asynchronous threaded discussions, in the fast-moving synchronous chat mode, it is difficult to enforce use of proper grammar and spelling. In fact, students and teachers may allow use of online chat acronyms or shortcut symbols as part of their netiquette (as shown in chapter 5). However, the time delay of the asynchronous threaded discussion mode allows students to reflect on and refine their personal responses to others' **posts**. Because of the time delay, the teachers encouraged their students to apply what they knew about the writing process to brainstorm, draft, and edit those responses or queries before posting them to the group.

While reading the novel and researching information for their route maps, students often had their own questions, which they could direct toward others in their learning community, both in the face-to-face classroom and in the online literature circles. The following sections show how the online literature circles provided a venue for teachers to embed assessments and apply proximal instruction strategies for scaffolding students' comprehension of the novel, its historical context, and the overall logic of the story of Huckleberry Finn.

Assessment Embedded to Foster Comprehension

Balazs and Drew generated a set of comprehension questions that individual students and the literature circle groups used to focus their discussions about the print novel and informational texts found online. Students received regular feedback from teachers about their comprehension of the novel and how they interpreted the historical information researched online. These assessment questions were embedded into the design of the unit to generate evidence of students' ongoing progress toward curriculum benchmarks and standards for analyzing and interpreting historical events and information sources.

Initially, students wrote individual responses to reading comprehension questions before sharing their understanding of sections of the novel in their literature circle discussions, and teachers gave them written feedback on the individual responses. The types of questions varied. Teachers elicited students' simple recall of significant events and plot elements before asking more critical reading questions that required students to reflect on characterization, predictions of further developments, and Twain's context for writing. For example, they used questions such as How did Huck and Jim meet? Why did Jim want to get to New Orleans? and Why did they decide to travel together? The teachers embedded assessment questions later in the unit to guide students' selection of research topics related to the Mississippi region they were studying, as shown:

St. Louis, MO

The population of Kansas (just west of Missouri) grew from 107,000 to 1,428,108 between 1860 and 1890. What does this tell you?

Cairo, IL

Where is it located? What was it named after? How does this relate to the comparison between Huck and Moses?

New Orleans

What role did this city have in the slave trade? What happened there during Reconstruction?

Students also took a more traditional final test about the novel, which included matching, short-answer, and essay questions. As the culminating assessment task, students created group route maps that illustrated and described their comprehension of the novel and the real-life historical context of major events in the novel. The route map directions required that students identify the importance of places the characters visit along the Mississippi River in conjunction with the real-life historical events that occurred there during the Reconstruction era. The primary goal of the route map was for students to demonstrate their comprehension of the characters and analysis of the Mississippi region during the Reconstruction period of U.S. history. Students submitted drafts of their route maps and teachers provided timely feedback on drafts to correct any student misconceptions or to prompt further reading or research.

The route map group projects were evaluated using the Route Map Rubric on page 45, which shows the criteria and rating scale teachers used to provide students with guidelines for developing and finalizing their route maps. The rubric covers the areas of content (i.e., quality of comprehension and research) and presentation (i.e., clarity, appearance, organization, and grammar and mechanics). In addition, teachers wrote detailed comments explaining the ratings they circled for each of these areas when evaluating students' drafts and final products. Students received a draft rating and used the rubric feedback from their teachers within their groups to guide revisions.

Applying Principles of Proximal Instruction

Initially, each literature circle was assigned one discussion question. Students were asked to discuss and agree on an answer and support it with details from the novel. They then shared their group answer with the whole class. Balazs spent time facilitating students' reading comprehension during the literature circle discussions, as shown in the online discussion excerpts. At the end of each assigned reading section, Balazs reorganized students into different groups to ensure that more students had the opportunity to contribute significantly to the literature circle discussions. This also provided students with opportunities to gain perspectives from a variety of their peers and challenged each student to express to the group his or her own autonomous thinking.

ROUTE MAP RUBRIC

Rating   Quality of Comprehension

0   No evidence of comprehending the historical significance of characters or themes in the novel and related historical trends in informational text

15   Some evidence of comprehending the historical significance of characters or themes in the novel and related historical trends in informational text

30   Extensive evidence of comprehending the historical significance of characters or themes in the novel and related historical trends in informational text

Comments:

Rating   Quality of Information Research

0   No evidence of valid research about six significant places and events in Huck Finn's personal journey and post–Civil War American society

15   Some evidence of valid research about six significant places and events in Huck Finn's personal journey and post–Civil War American society

30   Extensive evidence of valid research about six significant places and events in Huck Finn's personal journey and post–Civil War American society

Comments:

Rating   Clarity of Presentation

0   Unclear connections between the historical settings on the route map and major episodes in the novel

5   Somewhat clear connections between the historical settings on the route map and major episodes in the novel

10   Clear connections between the historical settings on the route map and major episodes in the novel

Comments:

Rating   Appearance and Organization of Presentation

0   Does not show organized geographical route of Huck and Jim's journey along the Mississippi River

10   Some inaccuracies shown in the organization of the geographical route of Huck and Jim's journey along the Mississippi River

20   Accurately shows well-organized geographical route of major events in Huck and Jim's journey along the Mississippi River

Comments:

Rating   Grammar/Mechanics of Presentation

0   Writing lacks use of proper grammar and mechanics

5   Writing needs improvement in grammar and mechanics

10   Writing adheres to proper grammar and mechanics

Comments:

Total Points and Overview Comments:

Literacy Learning in Networked Classrooms: Using the Internet With Middle-Level Students by Mary L. McNabb with Bonnie B. Thurber, Balazs Dibuz, Pamela A. McDermott, and Carol Ann Lee. Copyright © 2006 by the International Reading Association. May be copied for classroom use.

The first discussion questions posted online also were printed on the class handouts. Students could choose how to answer the question: in individual journal entries to be shared in face-to-face discussions or in the online literature circle. To get students started online, Balazs asked interested students to log on to the Collaboratory as a homework assignment one evening. He posted the following directions:

Participating in this book talk about Huckleberry Finn is a good way for sixth graders to become comfortable with the post and reply format. You may share ideas, ask questions, and discuss the novel, as well as share resources and ideas about the "Huck Finn Route Map" project. Please use proper grammar and mechanics (capitalize!).

Once the literature circles had moved to the asynchronous threaded discussion, teachers provided prompts to keep students focused on discussing the meaning of the novel. The teachers responded to students' posts with a variety of proximal instruction strategies to stimulate students' further analysis of aspects of the story. For example, in order to understand Huck's and Jim's separate motives for embarking on the journey down the Mississippi River, students were asked to explain the pressures acting upon each character and to perceive the characters' perspectives and attitudes. The following is an example of an online interaction designed to elicit students' understanding of the character Huck Finn.

Mr. Dibuz: How does Huck feel about being "sivilized"?

Lauren: Huck does not like being "sivilized" because the Widow Douglas does not let him do "fun stuff" like smoking, swearing, wearing dirty clothes, and skipping school and church. He does not want to live like society and the Widow Douglas wants him to.

Mr. Dibuz: Does Huck understand religion (Christianity)? Explain with examples.

Lauren: Huck does not understand Christianity fully. For instance, Huck said he did not want to go to the "good place." He wanted to go to the "bad place" because he thought the good place sounded boring. Also, Miss Watson told Huck that if he was good and helped others, he would get what he prayed for. Huck wished for a fishing line and fishing hooks. When he got the line but not the hooks, he decided prayer didn't work. Huck was interested in studying Moses, until he found out Moses was dead and then he no longer cared about him.

This online exchange between Lauren and her teacher, Balazs, illustrates how teachers can use online dialogue to assess individual students' comprehension through a question-and-answer cycle tailored for each student. Other students in the literature circle also benefit as they observe the exchange between their peer and teacher.

As appropriate, teachers also created direct links to supplementary informational text resources online that specifically guided students to investigate answers to history questions they posed to the teacher or peers in their literature circle. Balazs observed that some of the students who typically were reluctant to assert their interpretations or to ask questions in the face-to-face discussions were more responsive to the individual attention online. In addition, the possibility of linking to online resources in the same space made connections between the novel and its historical context more immediate for students.

Another strategy Balazs and Drew used to scaffold comprehension was asking students to make predictions about what would happen to the characters in the section of the book the students were about to read. Teachers can facilitate these types of question-and-answer sessions to help students plan, manage, and check their interpretation of what they read and guide their development as independent readers. These learning experiences also foster development of middle-level readers' comprehension monitoring, which is an intended outcome of proximal instruction.

Having a number of students pioneer the online literature circles gave the teachers the opportunity to monitor how students responded so they could adjust their instruction accordingly. Soon the discussions gained momentum that drew in other students, who joined with confidence after seeing how peers interacted. Most students were comfortable making the shift from face-to-face discussions to the online asynchronous threaded discussions. In fact, as the online discussions progressed, many students showed a greater level of comfort sharing their personal interpretations and asking their own probing questions about the novel than teachers had observed during the face-to-face discussions.

Online discussions tend to take on a life of their own with students often leading students. The following exchange illustrates how Balazs used the online discussion to prompt students to explore their own topics and how student perspectives sometimes steer online discussions:

Rebecca: During the night Huck and Jim were separated by an island and a heavy fog. Jim was on the raft and Huck was on the canoe. They whooped so they could find each other. Huck caught up with Jim in the morning when Jim was sleeping and made Jim think he was dead. Huck realized this was mean and decided not to do anything like this again. Huck respects Jim.

Mr. Dibuz: I think you are touching upon a very interesting theme in this discussion. I am especially interested in Huck's death. Not only is he dead in the eyes of society, but his assumed killer (Jim) is traveling with him. What might this say about the symbolic meaning of Huck and Jim's voyage? If it is about relations between whites and blacks, what could the "death" symbolize?

This prompt encouraged Rebecca to make connections between the events and themes in the story as well as the historical milieu, helping her develop strategies for interpreting the novel as a reflection of the social and political attitudes of the time. As a result, another student, Lauren, responded in greater detail, trying out a number of possible interpretations:

Lauren: Could death symbolize slavery? Or maybe not being able to live the way you would like to live. Do you think that people other than the widow Douglas, Tom, and Aunt Polly are mourning over the death of Huck? I think that the only reason that Jim is being searched for is because he supposedly committed TWO crimes. I do not think that very many people look upon Jim with compassion. Jim is a pretty good guy, but because he is black, hardly anyone bothers with him or even imagines him being important.

Initially, the teachers asked questions that were designed to help students focus on specific themes, which allowed their teachers to evaluate each student's basic comprehension of the novel. The dialogue exchange above shows how Balazs intentionally introduced more open-ended questions, which elicited evidence of more complex comprehension from students. For example, sometimes it was necessary to prompt students to move beyond the cause-and-effect answers associated with plot to a level of analysis of character motivation. The types of discussion strategies teachers used depended upon how well the students were progressing in their reading comprehension. The following teacher question concerning Huck's decision to reveal the scheme of the King and Duke illustrates a proximal instruction prompt Balazs used to scaffold Rebecca's comprehension beyond facts in the story so that she would think more deeply about character motivation.

Mr. Dibuz: What is important about the fact that Huck tells Mary Jane the "truth"? What does it foreshadow?

Rebecca: Telling Mary Jane the truth is important because it will catch the duke and the king. Huck's plan is to try to get away without the king and duke, and then have Mary Jane spread the news that they are frauds. He tells Mary Jane about the Royal Nonesuch, just in case everyone needs proof about the duke and king.
    Huck telling Mary Jane and no others foreshadows the return of the real uncles. Most people believe the duke and king, but some of them side with the real uncles. When questioned about the gold, the frauds repeat a story Huck used, about the slaves taking it. The frauds and the real uncles argue on, until it comes to the tattoo on Peter Wilkes' chest. They go to dig up the corpse and find the gold. The king and duke nearly win, because Mary Jane was away and could not tell everyone the duke and king were frauds. Meanwhile, Huck escapes. When he is leaving with Jim, the king and duke join him.

Although this thoughtful response shows that the student understood the actions in the story and could predict the most likely outcome, Balazs still wanted her to think even more analytically about Huck's feelings and what his actions in the story demonstrate about how he may have grown as a character. (Huck had been concerned earlier in the story about being culpable in the crime but had not spoken up about it.)

Mr. Dibuz: This is a good, detailed exploration of Huck's actions, Rebecca. Telling Mary Jane does reveal the plot (of the Duke and King), but what does it say about Huck and his willingness to help others and to put himself at risk by telling the truth?

Rebecca: What Huck telling Mary Jane the truth shows about Huck is that he really has a good heart. When Mary Jane was terribly sad he helped her, when he could have just supported the frauds and received a lot of money. It was very clever of him to come up with a plan that included Mary Jane. I think he as grown a lot since the beginning of the book. For instance, he didn't believe in G-d [God], but now, even though he doesn't think he believes in G-d, he acts like a follower of religion, being kind and trying to help any way he can.

Because Rebecca's initial response only explained a plot element, Balazs further prompted the student to interpret the events in terms of character development, which is a more complex task and an important reading skill.

One of the benefits of the online literature circles is that the dialogue about the novel moves from one of question and response between teacher and student to one of group exploration. Rather quickly and effectively, students themselves begin to ask questions and even to propose topics of discussion. The student-initiated **threads** can be as simple as asking for clarification or as ambitious as offering alternative interpretations of the text. What the students want to discuss about the novel does not matter so much as the fact that they are leading the academic discussion—which shows they are taking ownership of the online literature circle and value it. At one point in the discussion about the relationship between Huck and Jim, a student offered the following observation of his own:

thread:
A running log of asynchronous posts on the same topic.

Nigel: I pity Jim because Huck seems to be moving farther emotionally from him. Jim is becoming more and more like the assistant instead of the elder or friend. Anyone who wants to add or comment on this please feel free to. THANKS!

Sara: I agree with you Nigel. Jim is becoming more of an assistant. Huck seems to be regressing back to his old selfish ways. What has made Huck do this? Did his "time" with the Grangerfords transform him into something like them? Each Grangerford seemed to have a "personal slave," maybe this experience got to his head.

Sara went on to make a general observation based on her understanding of the literary device irony, which the class had learned about earlier in the unit.

Sara: Is Jim being affected at all by the changes Huck has been going through? Since we're the readers, things are more apparent to us than the characters. Do you think Huck is noticing his changes or is he oblivious to them?

Mr. Dibuz posted a series of follow-up questions to cultivate a more in-depth analysis among those participating in the student-initiated discussion and to tie this discussion to the overall class theme.

Mr. Dibuz: If you feel there is a change in Huck, show us with one or two examples what you mean exactly. Was Huck beginning to be more respectful to Jim before the Grangerfords? Was Huck happy to see Jim again? What exactly is he (Huck) doing that makes you say he does not treat Jim as well now? Anybody is welcome to share opinions here.

Lauren: Was it the Grangerfords' influence that is causing Jim to become more of an assistant? I think that is definitely a possibility. The Grangerfords lived (with the exception of the feud) like they were very important and high in society. I think that having his own personal slave at the Grangerfords changed how Huck looked upon Jim. Before Huck's stay with the Grangerfords, I thought that Jim was like a brother to Huck, but now Jim may seem more like someone who is around for Huck's inane, selfish ways. Do you think that if Jim were clumsy or lazy that he would still be sailing with Huck? I don't. I think that the first time Jim shows laziness or makes a mistake, like knocking supplies overboard by mistake, his chance of traveling with Huck for much longer will be pretty slim. Maybe I'm just not seeing the situation the way it really is. Are we underestimating Huck? Maybe the brotherly respect is just hidden.

Sara: I agree with Lauren. Jim's chances of staying on the river with Huck would be pretty slim if he made a mistake. Yet I'm not sure if Huck is hiding his "brotherly love." All siblings have disagreements, but since the story takes place during a time of slavery, it seems weird that a white boy is traveling down the river alone with a runaway slave. This especially seems weird because Jim is wanted for running away and the "killing" of Huck.

If you think about it, if you were a white boy traveling down the river with a runaway slave, wouldn't it feel kind of weird? Maybe we're overestimating Huck, not underestimating him. Maybe his love isn't really there. When Huck thought about turning Jim in, it made me think more and more that there was no love. But even though Huck didn't turn Jim in, was this only out of pity? At first, I thought Huck thought of Jim as a brother, yet this "unexpected" change has made me think differently. Maybe I'm looking at this the wrong way, but is the love really there?

Nigel: I think that Mark Twain is symbolizing the relationship between the whites and the blacks.

Lauren, who had been reading these exchanges, offered another interpretation.

Lauren: I thought that, like we talked about in class, Mark Twain is portraying two very different people who aren't looked upon very highly by society. Now I am not so sure. Since I think that we all agree that Huck's stay with the Grangerfords seems to have changed him, will Huck change his point of view about not caring what other people think and become one of the people who does and thinks like society wants him to because society wants him to? Is Huck turning into somebody society may come to accept and at the same time turning away from Jim? Mr. Twain has certainly created a plot that just keeps changing and becoming more complicated. When we first started the book, I thought that Huck would meet Jim; they would become best friends, sail to freedom, and celebrate. I thought that it would be so predictable, but they are definitely not best friends, and are sailing away from freedom! Plus the emotions that we see the characters going through are life-like. In a lot of books, the character has a perfect life, but in this book it seems more real.

Through these posts Balazs witnessed dramatic growth between the students' face-to-face and online dialogue. Students who hesitated to participate in face-to-face discussions were sharing their ideas and had original insights about the readings. Those who could not bring themselves to handwrite reflectively in their journals on a regular basis came into their own as literary critics when they observed peers posting original ideas during the online literature circles. This is how distributive learning communities operate. With teacher guidance, student exchanges become prolific at times. In this way, the Internet provides added value to developing students' comprehension and ownership of literacy. It is a facilitation tool for proximal instruction strategies that allows student peers to interact in new ways while teachers scaffold the development of their autonomy as literary critics.

Students worked together in pairs or groups of three to decide which six episodes from the novel they wanted to include in their route maps. The teachers gathered and evaluated sample paragraphs that individual students had written about one episode. The evaluations were returned to the groups, where they were shared and discussed so students would get as much feedback as possible before continuing to plan their route maps. As students wrote the text for their route maps, the teachers helped them develop their descriptions and interpretations more fully and also assisted in the proofreading and editing of the student work.

The following online discussion exchange is an example of the support students can receive online from teachers as they need help with specific aspects of their comprehension. By cross-referencing the plot of Huck and Jim's journey with the actual geography and historical context of their route, students were asked to demonstrate their comprehension of the novel on many levels. Sara, however, returned to the online literature circle with a question that had been bothering her. In return, Balazs provided her with a historical explanation to help resolve her confusion and misunderstanding of the novel.

Sara: Why did Jim want to get to Cairo? It was south of Missouri and he could have just tried to cross the Mississippi River somehow. This makes NO sense to me...

Mr. Dibuz: Glad to see you are asking for help here. Luck would have it that I am also online, so I will help out. First, you have to know that Jim had to get to Ohio to be in a free state. Second, they could only travel undetected on the rivers. So, the route would have to be: Mississippi to Cairo then Ohio (river) to Ohio. Illinois was, of course, a free state. OK, my next inclination is that some states had "fugitive slave laws," which meant they were under obligation to send slaves back to their states of origin (ownership, actually). I will now look this up.

Mr. Dibuz: [five minutes later] OK. I found it. I am quoting the text here, but look at the description of the "Fugitive Slave Act" of 1850 and especially how people in different parts of the North reacted to it. (excerpt from quote from website) "fugitive slave laws, in U.S. history, the federal acts of 1793 and 1850 providing for the return between states of escaped black slaves." It is likely that Illinois was known as a state that would return slaves, while Ohio and other northern states further east resisted the law and allowed slaves to run to Canada if necessary.

Sara's question above shows her misunderstanding of the Fugitive Slave Act as well as the use of rivers as the primary source of transportation during the 1800s. The explanation Balazs provided had more meaning because it responded to a perceived need that the student expressed with a real desire to improve her comprehension of the novel.

Balazs reflected on the nature of Sara's question and decided it was important enough to further discuss the Fugitive Slave Act orally with the whole class. The act of turning a student question into a history lesson represents a proximal instruction decision based on student feedback the teacher received. Sara felt comfortable enough to share her confusion online but may not have taken the initiative to ask her question orally in front of her peers. This is an excellent example of the added benefit of conducting literature circles online.

Showcasing Student Work

The culminating product, a route map, is a visual depiction of the group's comprehension of the novel's plot, its historical context, and the developing relationship between Huck and Jim. (See Figure 3 for a completed group route map.) The

FIGURE 3
Students' Completed Group Route Map

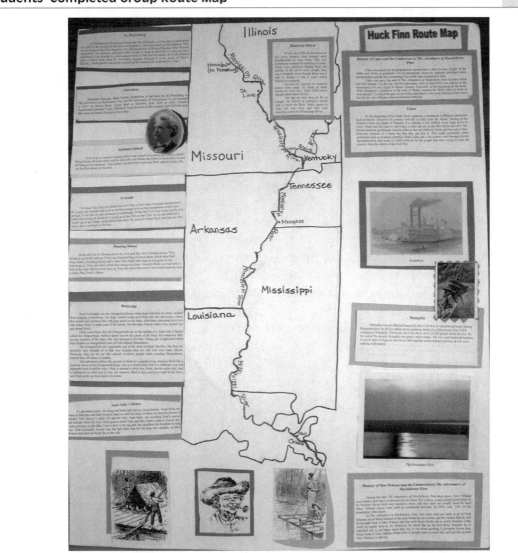

assessment task required students to write two paragraphs highlighting each of the six novel episodes and six historical events or places on their route maps. The following is an example of Lauren's parallel writings about an episode in the novel and the corresponding historical setting for the episode on the route map. In this route map example, Lauren described Jim's dilemma as he traveled with Huck down the Mississippi River toward New Orleans and explained her understanding of New Orleans during the 19th century.

Jim initially escapes from slavery because he hears that he is going to be sold down to New Orleans. New Orleans is the last place that Jim wants to be. If anyone sees him in New Orleans, he will be instantly put into an auction and sold, which means that he would probably never see his family again. Ironically, if Huck and Jim continue down the river, New Orleans is exactly where they will end up.

During the Nineteenth Century, New Orleans was a very important city. It had a huge port that was said to be the fourth best in the world. All of the goods that were shipped down the Mississippi river traveled to New Orleans, where they were transported around the world. New Orleans also received many imports from other countries. On top of that, the city was also a major hub for the slave trade, and thousands of slaves were taken away from their families at the auctions held there.

The juxtaposition of the two paragraphs on the map generates a visual representation of how students synthesized the literary and historical realms, furthering their comprehension and interpretation of the social–political conditions of the characters' lives during Reconstruction.

The final route maps took many shapes and involved a variety of media, from glue and paper to PowerPoint and other computer-generated—even interactive multimedia—presentations. Students were allowed to work in whatever medium was most comfortable for them so that they would not be hindered in sharing what they learned. The following is an example of student writing from the final essay test that shows the depth of comprehension sixth graders can achieve through participating in literacy learning activities such as Huck Finn's Journey.

New Orleans

Written by Lauren

In *Huckleberry Finn*, one important element in the plot is Jim's fear of being sold down river in New Orleans. During the Civil War Era, the black populace feared New Orleans because in that Louisiana city they were treated cruelly. There was a riot in New Orleans involving whites and blacks that some consider the bloodiest riot of that time. Over 30 people were killed and over 100 were wounded. Riots like these characterized relations between blacks and whites in the South. Most people at that time believed that it was wrong to help black people and that blacks should be treated as an inferior race. Society expected them to obey the Black Codes, a very strict set of rules that excluded blacks. Society said to think this way, and only a few people were able to ignore this and commit the "illicit" activity of helping blacks escape to freedom and other things that were bad and unlawful to society and the governments in the South. These people were called abolitionists.

In the novel, Huck protects Jim, a runaway slave, and the two run (or float) away together on a raft. A young white boy who is "un-sivilized" and a black man are on the same level in society. Huck and Jim soon bond and develop respect for each other, something many whites and blacks would and could not do. Unfortunately, Huck's type of affection and ignorance to social norms was in the minority, so there was not much hope for better relations between the whites and the blacks.

Lauren's writings show a variety of meaningful connections between the historical hypertexts and the literature she read and critically analyzed with peers in the online literature circle. In this regard, incorporating the **online literacy learning** activities into Huck Finn's Journey improved the degree of ownership students took in reading and interpreting the novel in its historical context, which greatly enhanced their comprehension of the story.

online literacy learning:
Reading, writing, and information research activities that occur via the Internet.

Conclusion

One of the greatest benefits of online literature circles is that students who are hesitant to share their ideas in face-to-face classroom discussions show a markedly greater freedom online in expressing their ideas and problems comprehending, which provides opportunities for teachers and others in the distributive learning community to scaffold their learning. Another benefit is that students who struggle to record their ideas by writing them manually on a piece of paper because of motor-skill problems may write more fluidly on the computer keyboard, and thus can participate without the frustration involved in putting pen to paper. In addition, once they are comfortable with the online discussion format, students start posting their own questions to challenge their peers, and some step in to coach others. In these ways, students learn to take ownership of their literacy.

Overall, the Internet brings various parts of the curriculum—such as discussing the novel, researching the period of history, composing the written elements of the route map, and, in some cases, creating the final product—into greater proximity. This, in turn, helps students synthesize their comprehension and critical analysis of both literature and informational texts. Conducting literature circles online tends to force students to take responsibility for their literacy learning requirements. If a student does not participate, teachers can notice it much more easily online. They can review archives of students' online participation levels and conduct follow-up interventions with students who are lagging behind expectations.

The degree to which students feel safe and comfortable sharing online is an indicator of how effectively the teachers have integrated the Internet into the learning environment. Getting students to read print materials such as books in the middle grades has become quite a challenge in networked cultures in which interactive texts abound. Once they learn how, students prefer to go online to conduct their literacy activities. For this reason, in the unit described in chapter 4 a teacher teamed up with a librarian to teach her students how to conduct online information research effectively.

GUIDING QUESTIONS FOR DISCUSSION

1. How did Balazs and Drew use the Internet to foster a community of literacy learners?

2. What proximal instruction strategies did these teachers use to address learning differences among students?

3. What types of online discussion questions can provide formative data about students' reading comprehension?

4. How can teachers design other online reading and writing assignments to foster students' ownership of literacy?

CHAPTER 4

Conducting Information Research Online

I have come to at least one conclusion from my many hours of observing students using the **Internet**: Middle-level students understand little about the literacy skills they need to be successful information researchers on the **World Wide Web**. Students who are novice information researchers assume it is easy to find information online. They are not aware that **search engines** cannot read for meaning. These students type questions directly into a search engine, expecting a human-like response, and do not realize they have to originate their own answer to the guiding research question for a project. If their question matches the subject of an online author, they may find a literal match at the top of their **search return list**, but more often that is not the case. Ask Jeeves, for example, is a search engine that queries an index of websites that have been compiled to give the illusion that it understands human questions, yet ask it a question that it is unprepared to answer and it cannot perform its magic.

Internet researchers attribute people's subconscious association of the Internet with social behaviors to its capacity to support human communications (Hermans, 1998; Wallace, 1999). However, the reality is that the Internet operates on programming languages, rather than natural human language, which presents computer programmers with a problem that they have studied for years. According to Hermans (1998), "it is not clear if it will ever be possible to make a computer fully understand natural language" (¶ 261). That is why it is important to provide students with opportunities to learn effective **search query strategies**, which typically include the use of keywords, operators, and synonyms or homonyms to help a search engine locate precise information efficiently. The more effective the query, the more efficient the search results will be.

However, according to Hermans (1997), locating information on the World Wide Web can be problematic even for expert searchers because "there is no central supervision on the growth and development of the Internet...and the dynamic nature

Internet:
Global infrastructure of information and communication networks.

World Wide Web:
Public portion of the Internet's online information resources.

search engine:
An online program used to index and access the contents of registered websites.

search return list:
A collection of Web resources compiled by a search engine.

search query strategies:
Purposeful combinations of keywords and operators used with a search engine.

of the information on the Internet changes without notice" (¶ 11). To complicate matters, none of the public search engines attempt to index the entire Internet. A single search engine catalogs only a fraction of the ever-changing billions of webpages (O'Neill, Lavoie, & Bennett, 2003). In addition, middle-grade students have difficulty distinguishing public websites from the **invisible Web**. Invisible Web resources tend to be of higher quality than resources found on the World Wide Web because more scrutiny goes into producing them. As a result, they may have greater educational value. An estimated 65% of Internet resources were housed on the invisible Web as of 2002, but the actual percentage is impossible to track. Invisible Web resources typically house their own search engines that only search through the resources hosted at their particular **domain**. School libraries may have online subscription databases as part of their invisible Web domain, but students may not find them if they are using a public search engine such as Google.

Different kinds of information formats and types of information services each require a unique search approach. For example, search engines typically scan only print unless the search query includes specific file types such as music, video, or graphics. In addition, novice researchers often do not read an online text thoroughly enough to truly comprehend and evaluate its context. Due to the **multisequential** nature of **hypertext**, information most pertinent to a student's research question may not appear at the top of the search return list or even on the homepage of a valuable website. However, middle-level students commonly click on the first **hyperlink** or two that a search engine finds, and if the answer is not readily apparent, they believe the information does not exist. They tend to use only this one strategy instead of multiple strategies, such as using a Web domain's site-specific search engine and the Web **browser's Find command** to help them scan online texts. Unless they are taught a variety of information research strategies to improve their online searching and critical reading, students go about asking natural language questions expecting the Web to resolve their research problem. This chapter focuses on how to prepare students to conduct effective information research online.

The Nature of Online Research

Conducting research online entails asking the right questions and staying focused to read for a specific research purpose. Successful online research requires students to apply a systematic research process to identify the research purpose, acquire keyword vocabularies for use in search queries, and develop skill at reading and evaluating informational text efficiently. Online, students will encounter persuasive arguments, expert opinions, and incongruent or unreliable evidence from a variety of sources. They will be confronted with the task of reading to understand the complexity of online contexts and analyzing multiple perspectives and their

invisible Web:
Online information not accessible to global search engines.

domain:
The Web address for an organizational or personal website.

multisequential:
Allows for diverse reading options in a single hypertext.

hypertext:
Digital print with hyperlinks readers click on to access other texts.

hyperlink:
Clickable text that connects to other hypertext or interactive multimedia.

browser:
An online interface used to access and read hypertext and interactive multimedia housed on the World Wide Web.

Find command:
A Web browser tool used to search a page for a word or phrase.

own biases before drawing conclusions about what they have read. They also face making decisions about if and how to apply information to solve a research problem. Students need to recognize when they require different or more information to satisfy their intended research purpose and have enough persistence to conduct additional search and critique cycles until they have evidence to sustain credible conclusions. In addition, students growing up in **networked cultures** need the technology skills to be able to use the World Wide Web as an effective information research tool. In short, they need **digital information literacy**. To learn more about digital information literacy methods and curriculum resources visit the suggested websites in Table 4.

As previously mentioned, Mitra's *Hole in the Wall Experiment* (Judge, 2000) demonstrates the ease with which students can learn from researching on the Internet when provided with a little guidance in their zone of proximal development. Mitra went to a middle class school in India, chose four 9th graders (two girls and two boys), and asked them to conduct online information research to answer 10th-grade test questions from their physics teacher. Mitra gave five questions on viscosity to the students, who did not have prior knowledge of the subject. The students had Internet access and two hours to find the answers to the questions, and they answered all questions correctly. For verification purposes, the physics teacher held a 30-minute discussion with the students and reported to Mitra that the students could explain their answers to the test questions. In addition, the students were able to tell the teacher several things about viscosity that the teacher did not know, but later verified as correct. Mitra explains,

networked culture:
A geographical community connected through Internet access to participants in the global village.

digital information literacy:
Ability to locate online, evaluate, and apply digital information.

TABLE 4
Digital Information Literacy Resources

www.kn.sbc.com/wired/21stcent/information.html
The Knowledge Network Explorer website, hosted by SBC Knowledge Ventures, is designed to help teachers and librarians effectively use the Internet in the information literacy curriculum.

www.big6.com
The Big6 information literacy model developed by Mike Eisenberg and Bob Berkowitz is sometimes referred to as a metacognitive scaffolding or an information problem-solving method.

www.noodletools.com/debbie/literacies/21c.html
The Tools for Reading the World webpage, hosted by NoodleTools, Inc., provides teachers with links to a variety of instructional approaches to develop students' 21st-century literacy.

Internet Tip: Websites shift in content and location periodically. Although care has been taken to list reliable websites, sometimes sponsors change or move webpages without notice to their readers. To find additional resource on this topic, conduct a keyword search at www.google.com or use your favorite search engine.

Keywords to Consider: *information literacy +research model +digital*

That's not a wow for the children, it's a wow for the Internet. It shows you what it's capable of. The slum children don't have physics teachers. But if I could make them curious enough, then all the content they need is out there. The greatest expert on earth on viscosity probably has his papers up there on the Web somewhere.... The teacher's job is very simple. It's to help the children ask the right questions. (¶ 16)

Mitra later states the point more explicitly,

I'm saying that, in situations where we cannot intervene very frequently, you can multiply the effectiveness of 10 teachers by 100- or 1,000-fold if you give children access to the Internet. (¶ 17)

I agree with Mitra to the extent that when students are well-prepared for this type of information research task, the Internet can be a useful learning environment for them. Certainly, well-designed research questions are important to guiding the information research process. Mitra's report also infers that his students were keen on identifying keywords in the test questions given to them. This ability to translate a natural language question into a search query is a significant information research skill. The rarer a keyword is, such as *viscosity*, the easier a search engine is able to locate pertinent information and present it at the top of the search return list. However, it takes more than a well-designed search task to be a successful learner online. The students who were selected for his study undoubtedly had good independent reading comprehension, or they would not have been studying physics in ninth grade. Furthermore, they worked in a group, which maximizes learning outcomes, as discussed in chapters 1 and 2. These are all factors in his students' successful learning experience.

Serious online research does not come as easily to most students in the middle grades, who often do not possess the reading and reasoning competencies to perform independent research online. For several decades, research has shown consistent problems associated with reading hypertext and **interactive multimedia** that affect how successfully students conduct online information research. Heller (1990) reviewed early interactive multimedia studies that were conducted during the 1980s and found indications of problems such as reader disorientation, cognitive overload, flagging commitment, and unmotivated rambling (sometimes called **surfing** the Web). Heller identified a browsing strategy, which is characterized by following links perceived to be relevant, as ineffective for novice information researchers and concludes that novices tend to be unable "to formulate a search objective and thereby be unable to take advantage of the richness of the [interactive multimedia] system" (p. 433). Subsequent research reviews indicate these early findings persist in more recent findings about the nature of reading hypertext and interactive multimedia texts (Kamil et al., 2000; Lockard & Abrams, 2004; Reinking & Bridwell-Bowles, 1996). In addition, online research

interactive multimedia:
Related multimodal information that can be presented together with hyperlinks.

surf:
To browse information on the Web leisurely.

also requires students to develop strong comprehension-monitoring and critical reading skills, which are discussed in more depth in chapter 2. As discussed in chapter 6, thoughtful design of online interactive curricula and appropriate scaffolding can help offset problems students may encounter with online texts.

InPormation Power ShiPt

In cyberspace, gone are the curriculum committees, librarians, and textbook editors who historically filtered all of the information coming into the classroom. These gatekeepers meticulously assessed the value and reliability of information before allowing it into classrooms, scrutinized the reading level, and categorized it accordingly. Before the Internet entered schools, students were given finite lists of information resources by their teachers and librarian that they could cite for their research projects. Teachers and librarians also read those resources. When conducting online research, however, the available resources are seemingly limitless. Judging the quality of online resources ultimately resides in the hands of each reader. This represents a shift in responsibility many educators fear giving to students, and for good reason. Certainly turning students loose on the Internet without supervision and appropriate instruction would be irresponsible because many middle-level students are unprepared for the challenges of online research. However, not preparing students to use the Internet as an information resource is no longer a viable option.

Purcell-Gates (1997), like many other literacy educators, gives voice to this dilemma:

> How are we best to instruct children in the managing of, contributing to, and using of the ever-expanding electronic information systems that dominate the workplace and other arenas of activity in the world today? How will we conceptualize language arts instruction in light of these demands? What skills and knowledge will learners need to successfully master this arena? (pp. 281–282)

McNabb and colleagues (2002) set out to address some of these questions. My colleagues and I found that because the Internet provides students with access to vast amounts of uncensored, interactive text at varying reading levels, teachers need to assist students in developing their independent reading, information evaluation, and synthesis skills. Teachers also can benefit from working with librarians on planning and implementing an online research initiative. In a series of studies, Lance and Loertscher (2005) have found consistent, strong correlations between students' reading achievement and the amount of time school librarians collaborate with teachers and students on research tasks including digital information literacy activities. School librarians, trained in information literacy standards (see www.ala.org), often provide students with a hands-on orientation to information research. With guidance about how to formulate a research question, use an Internet search engine efficiently, and evaluate texts according to a research purpose, students can learn to forge their own reading paths that link their prior knowledge to their curiosity about a topic.

collaborative learning environment:

A password-protected workspace for groups.

networked classroom:

Environment in which students and teachers use the Internet for educational purposes.

This type of collaboration occurred between Pam McDermott, a middle school librarian, and Mary Fran McBreen, a health teacher, who teamed up to redesign an existing 10-day unit on the study of human body systems to include online research. Unlike the teachers in chapter 3, who had the privilege of using a password-protected **collaborative learning environment**, Pam and Mary Fran demonstrate how to turn the World Wide Web into a safe and effective curriculum resource for students. Figure 4 identifies the unit's features aligned with the framework for organizing **networked classrooms** as discussed in chapter 1.

FIGURE 4
Characteristics of Learning Opportunities in the Understanding Human Body Systems Unit

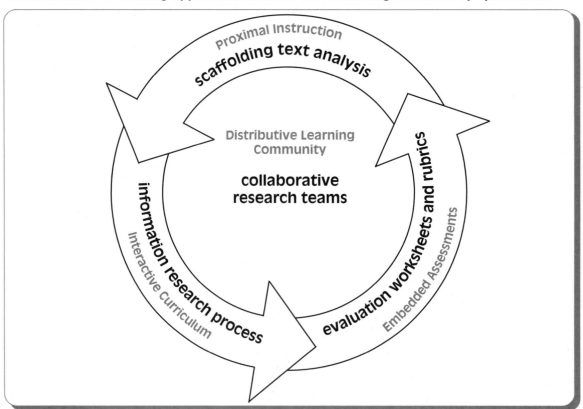

Understanding Human Body Systems

Curriculum Objective: To scaffold students' information research process, including online strategies for locating and evaluating hypertexts and interactive multimedia information through collaborative research teams.

Materials: A.D.A.M. (interactive multimedia software for studying life sciences in grades 5–8); *Family Health Encyclopedia* CD-ROM (an interactive multimedia reference guide to common ailments and general practices for good health); **interactive whiteboard**; list of preselected hoax and reliable medical websites.

Time Frame: Two weeks

Technology Standards: Addresses NETS-S (ISTE, 1999) under the categories technology research tools and technology productivity tools.

interactive whiteboard: A wall-mounted projection screen with touch sensors that control a computer.

Design of the Interactive Curriculum

Mary Fran and Pam set out to update an existing unit, Understanding Human Body Systems, by including online information research activities on the World Wide Web. The unit had been a part of the health science seventh- and eighth-grade (cross-grade) curriculum for years, and during that time only print resources and CD-ROM encyclopedias had been accessible to students. However, those library resources were becoming outdated, and the Internet offered more current and less costly access to information. In addition, Mary Fran wanted to integrate online information into students' research activities because she felt a strong conviction to prepare her students for their future, which will require digital information literacy. Recognizing her own weakness in using the Internet, Mary Fran turned to Pam, the school librarian, for assistance. Pam has found that today's young adolescents compulsively choose the Internet as their sole research tool. She also has observed that middle-level students tend to believe the Web has the answers to all their questions and that attempts to prevent them from using their research tool of choice only causes disengagement from schooling. Pam is quick to point out, however, that using the Web for information research needs to be balanced with a variety of materials. *Books first, then online database subscriptions, then public websites* is her motto.

During the Understanding Human Body Systems unit, Pam and Mary Fran prepared students to effectively locate and evaluate online information resources for inclusion in a health science project, for which students study human anatomy. The intended outcome for the unit is for students to be able to explain the purpose and function of each of the 10 human body systems and how these systems interact with one another, and to identify and describe the effects of health-related risky behaviors. Mary Fran and Pam also aligned their revised unit with the NETS-S (ISTE, 1999) and with the Information Literacy Standards for Student Learning (see www.ala.org/ala/aasl/aaslproftools/informationpower/informationpower.htm) for efficiently and effectively accessing information, critically and comprehensively evaluating information, and accurately and creatively using information. They envisioned that the unit would facilitate students' becoming independent learners and contributors to the class learning community. As part of their own professional development, Pam and Mary Fran studied internationally recognized models for information literacy (American Association of School Librarians & Association for Educational Communications and Technology, 1998), information research (Eisenberg & Berkowitz, 2000), and the information-seeking process (Collier, 2004).

Pam and Mary Fran had to find a solution for dealing with an Internet filter that blocked websites they wanted their students to access for this unit. Their district's website filtering software was sensitive to the subject matter their students were researching—the human body. Turning the filter off was not an option. Instead, they met with the district administrator in advance to explain the content of their unit. They took to the meeting a list of credible websites and made the case for why their students needed access to information online about the human reproductive system. Together with the district administrator they decided on a filter management strategy to provide their students with access to relevant websites. The particular website addresses they had chosen for the unit were added to the filter's "safe websites" category.

School communities often adopt a combination of electronic filtering and Internet usage policies that carry consequences for students' misbehavior to manage access to public Web resources. Under Pam's recommendation, her school also bought subscriptions to password-protected websites. These are measures to meet the requirements of the U.S. Congressional Children's Internet Protection Act (CIPA) in 2001. Critics argue that protection measures, such as filtering or blocking software, do not adequately achieve the goal of protecting minors from obscenity, child pornography, and other harmful material and fundamentally violate First Amendment rights (Johnson, 2001). Filters often block valuable curriculum resources, but teachers can work around them if they are aware of how they function. (See *The Librarian's Guide to Great Web Sites for Kids*, www.ala.org/ala/pio/availablepiomat/librariansguide.htm, sponsored by the American Library Association, to learn more about online protection practices.) Pam and Mary Fran successfully dealt with the challenge of giving their students opportunities to learn how to search and evaluate information so they would become wise information consumers by working with the district's Internet filter.

Well-designed information research activities typically help students focus their purpose from the onset. For example, the purpose may be to assist in solving a particular problem, to become informed about a specific issue, or to answer an important question. There are many purposes for conducting information research. Among those applicable to middle-level students are comparing and contrasting expert opinions, expanding understanding of trends, and exploring multiple perspectives on a topic. In the Understanding Human Body Systems unit, students are required to articulate in writing their research purpose. This activity provides students with a focus shaped by their own interests, prior knowledge, and curiosity about the human body.

Pam and Mary Fran had learned through experience that one of the most effective ways to teach students how to manage their online information research process is to chunk the project into manageable steps. They set specific goals for each step in the research process with hands-on group time for students to work in depth on each step. They also had students use daily graded **log** sheets for their time online, which helped keep the students focused on their research purpose, and worksheets that required students to answer questions and take notes, which promoted serious research efforts. The sequence of learning activities for the unit is outlined in Table 5.

Students began their information research using the library's print and CD-ROM resources described in Table 5. Once they completed assigned worksheets

log:
An automated record of Internet activity.

TABLE 5
Understanding Human Body Systems Curriculum Activities

Sequence	Events
Day 1	Teacher and students engage in an interactive discussion about students' prior knowledge and initial questions, unit expectations, and overview of the research process and guiding research question for the unit. A criterion-referenced pretest is administered.
Days 2–3	Students design individual learning plans for their unit of study using a research organizer worksheet and preview a collection of science and medical books, CD-ROM software such as A.D.A.M. (interactive anatomy and multimedia software for studying life sciences in grades 5–8) and the *Family Health Encyclopedia* CD-ROM (an interactive multimedia reference guide to common ailments and general practices for good health), and online subscription database resources compiled by the teacher and librarian.
Days 4–6	The librarian and the teacher team teach basic Internet search strategies and an in-depth hoax website lesson using an interactive whiteboard, website evaluation worksheet, and a preselected list of websites—some of which are hoax websites with unreliable information. Students are required to compare the websites from the list by applying information evaluation criteria. Student pairs also brainstorm search terms and use terms to locate online information about their chosen body system at their own pace.
Day 7	Students complete a formative objective test covering human body system content aligned with health education and science standards.
Day 8	Students collaborate on organizing their group writing and presentation in response to the guiding research question and support their answers with information from properly cited sources.
Days 9–10	Student groups make class presentations and write group reports using one of five formats. They individually complete a criterion-referenced posttest of content aligned to the specified standards. The combination of written work and test results requires each student to demonstrate his or her understanding of human body systems, how these systems work in unison, and how risky behaviors affect different systems in the body.

about different human body systems and Mary Fran verified they had ample background knowledge about the basic function of each body system, she allowed them to begin focusing on the unit's guiding research question:

Is one body system more important than any of the others?

Mary Fran and Pam took care structuring the guiding research question to prompt students to examine and discuss among themselves how the 10 systems work together in the body. The question required student teams to solve a problem using inferential thinking skills. During instruction, these teachers brainstormed with students to imagine what would happen if one of the body systems went missing. Students learned that researching information alone would not answer their guiding questions. They researched in order to become more informed but had to pose for themselves their own hypotheses and ultimately present a case based on their findings and conclusions. As part of their research, students were required to verify and cite their facts from at least three different types of sources (e.g., books, periodicals, software or websites). Student groups were required to present evidence for their answers to the guiding question during their final presentations.

Organizing the Distributive Learning Community

During the pilot of the upgraded unit, Mary Fran observed that many middle-level students were not mature enough to handle independent research using the Web, so she began grouping them. She has concluded that in order to keep students on task during their time online, it is essential to have a team strategy. Within each class group, she organized students' learning activities in several ways. Students were assigned to small groups of five or six for their overall study of the Understanding Human Body Systems unit. Within each group, students decided upon their roles and responsibilities with regard to investigating all 10 body systems, at-risk health behaviors, and how the systems interact. Each student took responsibility for personally studying at least 2 of the 10 body systems and making judgments and inferences about the body system and how important it is to the other body systems. Students had to do their information research on an individual basis. Instruction then became one on one in the library's computer lab, with emphasis on individual students and their specific learning needs. For some of the lessons within the unit, such as brainstorming search terms, students were organized into teams of two for pair sharing.

In order to complete the Understanding Human Body Systems unit, student groups had to establish their own research purpose, which included defining their research focuses, information resources, and research tasks and managing their own research schedules within project deadlines. Mary Fran and Pam observed that students tended to remain on task because the project is individualized, authentic, and interesting. Each student was accountable for a group contribution. The temptation to copy or dawdle was reduced because each student had his or her own responsibilities. They collaborated with peers in putting together a comprehensive human body systems presentation that addressed the research purpose of discovering how the 10 primary body systems function together as a whole.

Assessment Embedded to Facilitate Knowledge Building

The Understanding Human Body Systems unit was designed to encourage students to assess their individual and group research accomplishments as well as to obtain formative feedback from their teacher. In their research packets, students were provided with the Understanding Human Body Systems Presentation Rubric (see page 68), which identifies the criteria for evaluating the presentation of their research. Students could format their presentation as a brochure, newspaper article, skit, TV commercial video, or as PowerPoint slides. Students were encouraged to refer to the rubric to guide their development of the presentations before Mary Fran used it to grade their group presentations. They also used the Learning Community Evaluation Rubric (see page 69) to rate their own and one another's contributions to the group. Mary Fran used these rubrics to foster students' equitable participation within the group. For quality control of the students' evaluation results, she determined through experience, it is best to drop the highest and lowest peer evaluation ratings for each student.

In addition, Mary Fran administered an existing criterion-referenced test before and after students conducted their information research. The test measured students' knowledge and skill aligned to content standards for understanding human body systems. Mary Fran used the pretest results to inform her instruction and to debrief students about areas in which they needed to focus their research to address their common misconceptions. Student worksheets were assessed in a timely manner during the unit's lessons to guide their investigating and knowledge building over the course of the 10-day research process.

Applying Principles of Proximal Instruction

Pam routinely scaffolds students' understanding of copyright and fair use of information by explaining these concepts at the beginning of each school year with every grade in her middle school when the English language arts classes come to the library. As part of their library visit, students complete in-depth units about cheating, copyright, and plagiarism. For sixth graders, she provides a basic explanation of what was considered cheating in their school regarding testing, homework, writing papers, and generating ideas. The seventh- and eighth-grade units build on students' prior knowledge. After reteaching these basic concepts of fair

UNDERSTANDING HUMAN BODY SYSTEMS PRESENTATION RUBRIC

Name of student research group:

Rating   Quality of Information Research—Human Body Systems

0   No evidence of accurate information researched and cited about the purpose and functions of the 10 human body systems.

15   Some evidence of accurate information researched and cited about the purpose and functions of the 10 human body systems.

30   Extensive evidence of accurate information researched and cited about the purpose and functions of the 10 human body systems.

Comments:

Rating   Quality of Information Research—Health-Related Risky Behaviors

0   No evidence of accurate information researched and cited about health-related risky behaviors and the consequences of risk-taking behaviors directly affecting each body system.

15   Some evidence of accurate information researched and cited about health-related risky behaviors and the consequences of risk-taking behaviors directly affecting each body system.

30   Extensive evidence of accurate information researched and cited about health-related risky behaviors and the consequences of risk-taking behaviors directly affecting each body system.

Comments:

Rating   Appearance and Organization of Presentation

0   Does not illustrate how the 10 human body systems interact with one another.

15   Some inaccuracies in the illustrations of how the 10 human body systems interact with one another.

30   Accurately illustrates how the 10 human body systems interact with one another.

Comments:

Rating   Grammar/Mechanics of Presentation

0   Writing lacks use of proper grammar and mechanics.

5   Writing needs improvement in grammar and mechanics.

10   Writing adheres to proper grammar and mechanics.

Comments:

LEARNING COMMUNITY EVALUATION RUBRIC

Name of Rater:

Name of Student Evaluated:

Learning Community Evaluation Criteria:

Points To organize our teamwork to complete tasks on time, I/or teammate
- 1 ☐ did not cooperate with my teammates.
- 2 ☐ cooperated with difficulty.
- 3 ☐ cooperated with ease most of the time.
- 4 ☐ cooperated with consistent ease.

While researching my topic, I/or teammate
- 1 ☐ was constantly off task.
- 2 ☐ was occasionally off task.
- 3 ☐ was on task throughout the project.
- 4 ☐ was on task as group leader.

For our group presentation, I/or teammate
- 1 ☐ did not contribute accurate information.
- 2 ☐ contributed unsatisfactorily.
- 3 ☐ contributed satisfactorily.
- 4 ☐ contributed in an exemplary manner.

I / _____ (or teammate's name)
- 1 ☐ did not complete the assigned role within the group.
- 2 ☐ completed the role unsatisfactorily.
- 3 ☐ completed the role satisfactorily.
- 4 ☐ completed the role in an exemplary manner.

Total Points

use, Pam explains the concept of "common knowledge" to seventh graders as well as the use of photos and online resources. Before students are introduced to citation formats, she conducts a question-and-answer, or a pretest, session about their understanding of the different issues. In this way, students are fully aware of the copyright and fair use rules and issues when they come to the library's computer lab to use the Internet for their research on human body systems. However, Pam consistently observes that when they are working on the Internet, all prior knowledge seems to evaporate. They do not always make the connection between using online resources and copyright restrictions. As a result, Pam finds it is essential for librarians and teachers to reinforce these concepts continually. By eighth grade the students not only must begin to understand copyright and plagiarism but also are expected to use correct citation formats.

With one group of students from Mary Fran's class, Pam simulated the information research process by conducting a series of online searches with student groups using the interactive whiteboard to display the results at the front of the class. She started with a topic and preselected the search terms to make certain she could get the results she wanted using Google (www.google.com) to demonstrate her key points. She prompted students to provide her with terms to refine their search on the same topic using a specific domain. Pam conducted the next search looking for information only housed on sites with the .edu domain. She concluded the simulation by exploring the search return list with the students and discussing why the domain-specific search provided better information resources than those found using other domains (such as .com or .org) in the domain. With prompting, the students easily could find the author, date, and copyright markings for their citation list on the educational websites. Pam also showed the students how to use online citation tools, for example, the one hosted by the Illinois Mathematics and Science Academy at http://21cif.imsa.edu, and pointed out the information that needed to be included in order to fulfill copyright requirements. To demonstrate her point further, Pam had students compare website citation information using the same citation format to see which sites lacked appropriate copyright and credibility. Following this instructional session, Pam monitored and scaffolded students' practice conducting online searches in the library's computer lab.

Translating the Research Question Into Searchable Terms. Teaching students to research information online efficiently and effectively is a complex process, as discussed earlier in this chapter. Information posted on public websites can be highly commercialized, biased, or inaccurate. In the open-publishing forum of the Internet, students need to be astute information searchers and analysts to sort through the vast web of online resources to find credible and reliable information. Teaching them to use a variety of search strategies helps them find the most relevant information within reasonable time limits. Organizing online searches into manageable chunks is an important goal-setting strategy used during proximal instruction to assist students in focusing their time.

Pam and Mary Fran use both prescriptive and descriptive scaffolding strategies, discussed in chapter 2, to monitor and guide students' online information research, which is inherently self-directed. Online, students can follow their own logic and train of thought as long as they are productive. During online research time, instruction becomes more meaningful because teachers and librarians are able to observe when a student's research process brings him or her to a dead end and can negotiate with the student a plan for evaluating the results of individual search tasks. Through their one-on-one interactions with teachers, students can raise personal questions they may harbor about their progress developing their research skills as well as technology literacy. Pam and Mary Fran can then interact in conversations that help the student to understand specific search strategies and results, including analysis of the publishing source and credibility of information. When a teachable moment or a breakthrough in learning occurs with a student, Pam emphasizes it to the entire class by demonstrating the minilesson using the interactive whiteboard. As students become comfortable with their own online research processes and confident in their emerging skills, they begin to take on the role of peer tutor. Pam has seen this progression with students repeatedly.

When students have difficulty generating effective search terms from their guiding research question and background knowledge of a human body system, they also may struggle with ways to combine terms that will produce the best search returns. Once online they might also forget their research purpose and simply surf the Web. For beginners in the online research process, it helps to provide them with a scaffolded opportunity to brainstorm about search terms using keyword vocabulary from the content area under study. Figure 5 shows an example of the search terms one student group identified during a brainstorming activity for the Understanding Human Body Systems unit. These terms are a good starting point and derived from students' background reading on the topic of the various body systems.

During the Understanding Human Body Systems unit, Pam prompted students to enter the keywords from their worksheets into the search engine. In order to refine their online search about a particular body system, Pam demonstrated on the interactive whiteboard how to scan the annotations of websites in the search return list to glean additional keywords that they could use to refine the next search queries. Students could use this effective information research strategy to learn more about their topic as they delved deeper into the research process. Effective search queries use operators (+ and – symbols) to expand or narrow the scope of a search and quotation marks for inclusive phrases. Pam insists on teaching students how to use operators even though some search engines will insert them automatically. Successful online researchers also learn

FIGURE 5
Body Systems Vocabulary Worksheet Sample

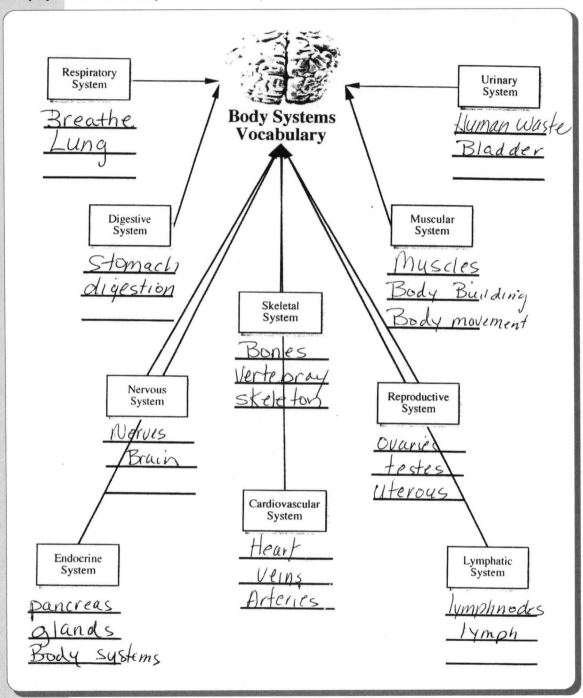

synonyms, homonyms, or antonyms for keywords they find in the search return list and combine these as a string of keywords in search queries that can locate pertinent Web resources efficiently.

Evaluating Online Information: Is It a Hoax? Pam believes that authentic research experiences for students must include exposure to unreliable information resources. She does so to create a teachable moment, in which she can guide students as they apply evaluation criteria to online information resources. When introducing online research methods to middle-level students, Pam typically requires online subscription databases as a starting point. For students working on the Understanding Human Body Systems unit, Pam and Mary Fran decided to try something new. They designed a hoax website lesson to demonstrate to students the unpredictability of what they may find when conducting research on the World Wide Web. The lesson focused students' attention on applying website evaluation criteria to a list of websites Mary Fran and Pam compiled. The websites listed are a mixture of reliable sources with accurate information and sources with gross inaccuracies. Table 6 lists some of the hoax websites students tend to believe are credible from Mary Fran's official website list. Their goal with the hoax website lesson is to enhance the seventh and eighth graders' research skills and information literacy by guiding them to assess the accuracy and credibility of the information.

To give students a frame of reference, Pam told them a story about a project turned in several years ago by a student. He had researched inventors, and the facts presented in his paper were acquired from a website. However, the Web source he chose was written by another sixth grader in Pennsylvania whose information was inaccurate. As a result, he received a poor grade. If he had tried to verify the information with a minimum of two other sources as directed, the student would have discovered the inaccuracy of his original source. After telling the story, Pam revisited a previous lesson about using synonyms and operators for

TABLE 6
A Sample of Hoax Websites

www.firstgenetics.com
The First Genetics research laboratory has an undisclosed location (in England), which is a hint students often overlook when evaluating the source of a website.

www.malepregnancy.com
The First Male Pregnancy website typically fools students with the quality of its website design and graphics.

www.geocities.com/TelevisionCity/Network/9000
The Clones R Us website presents a narrative story line that appeals to the imagination of students in ways that often prevent them from seeing the hoax.

narrowing a search result. Then, using the whiteboard Pam introduced a hoax website and, with students, examined the different criteria on the website evaluation worksheet (see Figure 6). As a whole class, they explored a website and looked for clues to answer the questions on their worksheet. Then the students were given time for guided practice comparing and evaluating two websites of their choosing from Mary Fran's official website list to determine if both sites were credible or not. Half the sites on the list were legitimate, and the others were hoaxes, but students were not told which ones. Pam discussed students' findings with them and explained that some websites intend to confuse and deceive readers. She wrapped up the lesson by explaining the information selection process that librarians use as well as checks and balances used in the publishing industry to evaluate information before it is published in print. These criteria are not always applied online, so when conducting information research online, students need to engage in the same screening process.

FIGURE 6
Student Website Evaluation Worksheet Sample

Website Evaluation Questions	Nate's Response	Mary Fran's Answer Key
Is there an introduction that tells you what the site is about?	No	Yes, there is an introduction; it is about how to get a personal clone.
How is this information useful for your project?	Its not. It just to buy clones	Correct; it's not applicable.
How do you know this site is or is not recognized by others as significant?	Because it's a geocitie link	Geocities sites may or may not be reliable; this one says it's a joke.
Does the author use strong OPINION words?	No, talks about useless things.	Allegedly trying to sell something; uses biased language such as "finest DNA" available.
How can you tell if the rest of the information is fact or opinion?	You really cant tell because it just advertisements	Yes, advertisements are a clue that it could be biased.
Pick one fact and write it here. Verify this fact in another website or book. List your source(s).	There was actually one sheep cloned before. Yes it was true	Not applicable*
Would you have gotten more information in an encyclopedia?	Yes, on clones	Yes, the encyclopedia would be more reliable than this website.
What can you conclude about this site?	That it serves no actuall point.	This is a hoax website.

*Mary Fran learned from Nate's response to this question and had to update her answer key accordingly.

Mary Fran collected and graded students' initial website evaluations using her answer key. Students completed a series of these worksheets and tended to improve their performance as they learned from the answer key feedback on graded worksheets. Figure 6 shows an example from a student's initial review of a website called Clones R Us, using the website evaluation worksheet developed by Mary Fran and Pam. At the beginning of the activity, the student, Nate, was unaware that the site was a hoax. From the results of his initial review, he decided the information was not useful to him, but he did not discredit the site altogether. One of the facts he found on the site (regarding scientists' claims to have cloned a sheep) he verified as true by checking another source. If he had read through more of the webpage, he would have read that the site's authors posted a disclaimer and acknowledged the site as a joke. Mary Fran also benefited from the process: On Nate's worksheet, she discovered an error in her answer key and learned something new from her student. Online information research is a complex endeavor, complicated by the capacity of hypertext to displace the reader's sense of context. The hoax website lesson is a prime example of how to scaffold students' understanding of the importance of reading thoroughly the context in which information appears online.

Students continued to use the Web evaluation worksheets to collect their notes about other sites they reviewed from the assigned website list, which included credible sites with information about human body systems. Mary Fran also kept track of the websites students cited in their reports and addressed any misconceptions they exhibited with regard to information found online. An interesting side effect of this approach is that these students discussed the hoax website lesson in other classes. After the pilot lesson, Pam was inundated with requests for training about phony websites from her colleagues—many teachers were as uninformed about how to recognize a deceptive website as were students.

Reflecting on the inclusion of the Internet in library research projects, Pam stated that the most important effect of students' learning experience during the Understanding Human Body Systems unit is their ability to question. Many times, students remain silent for fear of being embarrassed by asking a question, but when they learn to conduct research online, they know they can ask questions and often find resources to provide credible answers. Students learn how to make meaning from a greater variety of text formats such as video, sound file, graphics, maps, photographs, opinion polls, and so forth. They get excited about *using* information to generate knowledge, and their results are more creative than their old "invention" reports, according to Mary Fran. In addition, Pam notices students becoming faster learners in the library as they read in different ways for different purposes. The unit requires students to analyze and synthesize the information they research, rather than simply to retell facts or present expert opinions from published works. They truly develop a deep understanding and knowledge about the human body systems they study.

Student Showcase

The information research tasks required students do something with the knowledge they gained. Synthesizing information researched online is another crucial step in the research process. During the Understanding Human Body Systems unit, student groups presented the synthesized results of their research to their peers and teacher. Some used PowerPoint presentation software, while others use printed posters with illustrations or diagrams of the different body systems they obtained from credible medical websites. One group enacted a skit they wrote about the chain reaction effects of at-risk behaviors on different body systems. Because the online information research process does not result in inert knowledge, students may not always draw accurate conclusions. When two students from different groups presented the following information, Mary Fran thought at first they might have to revise their work:

Kalena: Your peripheral nervous system is made up of two types of neurons: sensory neurons and motor neurons. Sensory neurons run from receptors to the brain and inform it of the stimuli. Motor neurons run from the brain to the muscles and glands and send signals about certain actions that have to be taken. Messages from the brain are transmitted from nerve to nerve by jumping over the spaces between them, called dendrites.

Nate: There are three different types of neurons that occur. Sensory neurons that have a long dendrite and short axon and carry messages from sensory receptors to the central nervous system. There are motor neurons that have a long axon and short dendrites and transmit messages from the central nervous system to the muscles or some times glands. There is also interneurons that are found only in the central nervous system where they connect neuron to neuron.

Because their information was incongruent, Mary Fran requested that the students identify their sources, and both pointed to Internet websites. As a class, they reviewed the medical websites' information and discovered that both students actually were correct. Nate had researched the topic in more detail, following his innate curiosity about the research topic. Kalena focused more on the peripheral nervous system. Both perspectives were acceptable and in line with the unit's rubric criteria for content matter.

Mary Fran took class time to investigate the discrepancies between the two student reports to demonstrate to students their ethical responsibility when researching online. She also learned something new in the process. The ability to cut and paste or download information from authors unknown to teachers has made it easy for students to plagiarize. Pam believes it takes constant reteaching to emphasize the point that online information is not free for students to use without crediting the author and source, nor is it all reliable. Middle-level students may fail to credit the distinction between their own reports and the intellectual property and copyrights of other authors. Pam and Mary Fran overcome this obstacle with direct instruction, followed by guided practice sessions in which they scaffold students' development as information researchers.

Conclusion

The way Pam and Mary Fran designed and implemented the online research assignments within the Understanding Human Body Systems unit is a valuable example of how to introduce in-depth content area reading to young adolescents. The Internet is steeped in informational and expository texts generated for authentic purposes in the real world. If the same texts were assigned as printed reading materials, however, students might not be as interested or motivated to study them. However, because reading on the Internet is essentially a learner-centered process, it allows students to explore topics in as much detail as they desire. The hypertext links on the Web allow students to construct their own narratives within and across topics, but students need guided practice to learn how to stay focused on their research purpose as they search through the volumes of information online. They also need to develop critical reading skills for making meaning from the oftentimes meandering associations between hypertext links. Students who struggle with critical reading may show signs of particular difficulty during online information research activities, which was discussed in more depth in chapter 2.

The middle grades are an ideal time to scaffold the development of students' information research skills and associated thinking processes because of their natural curiosity about the world. The middle grades are also a good time to instruct students in how to be astute information consumers in the **global village**. Without the proper learning opportunities, students may develop harmful habits such as cutting and pasting information from Internet sources into projects without pausing to consider its reliability or to cite its source. Worst yet, they might continue surfing the Web without learning how to search efficiently or to evaluate information effectively. The health science unit presented in this chapter illustrates how adding an online research component to a unit can help students develop their content area vocabulary, comprehension of informational text, and critical thinking skills. Chapter 5 demonstrates how to support students' writing development online, another vital literacy skill for those growing up in the global village.

global village:
Networked cultures around the world connected via the Internet.

GUIDING QUESTIONS FOR DISCUSSION

1. What is the role of search engines, online database subscriptions, and online search techniques within an information research model or curriculum?

2. How can teachers and librarians collaborate to design online information research tasks that provide students with access to reading materials appropriate to academic content areas?

3. How can teachers assess students' online research processes, including where they went online, what information they gathered, and how long it took them to find it?

4. What is the teacher's role in fostering a community of learners who can demonstrate the ability to evaluate online information and synthesize and create reliable knowledge from their collective information research efforts?

CHAPTER 5

Learning the Writing Process Online

One day when I stepped into a middle-level classroom involved in a laptop initiative, I observed a group of students passionately typing away at their keyboards. I watched in awe of their intense concentration on their writing until the teacher informed me that he had just lost control of the students, who were not engaged in an assignment but rather misbehaving. Some giggled as they participated in a relay of **instant messaging** while others had initiated **synchronous chat** sessions with their friends. The teacher obviously was flustered by the situation. What he did not yet realize was that students had spontaneously formed a distributive learning community. Rather than fretting, he could learn how to organize their exploration of online writing to teach them valuable writing techniques and enhance their engagement in literacy acts applicable to their **networked culture**. While I empathize with the teacher's lack of preparation to scaffold their online writing to make it academically productive, I admire the students for taking ownership of an opportunity to learn how to communicate online.

The interactive nature of online dialogue is much different than dialogue in the nonnetworked classroom, a topic addressed in depth in chapter 2. Dialogue online distributes authority among its participants. Online dialogue is written and participatory, which can make it particularly useful for teaching students the writing process. Online, everyone has a voice and space to express it. **Internet** communication tools such as instant messaging, synchronous chats, and **asynchronous threaded discussions** can be used to structure interactions among student writers throughout the stages of the writing process. Online communication tools visualize individual students' writing processes for teachers to analyze and scaffold in personalized ways. Online, teachers can engage students individually and in groups in ways that enable students to understand their own unique writing abilities, perspectives, and selves more fully. Online learning communities can support students' development in ways unattainable in nonnetworked classroom settings where individual differences, interests, and abilities often go unnoticed.

instant messaging:
One-on-one online dialogue in real time.

synchronous chat:
Real-time exchange of online dialogue between multiple participants.

networked culture:
A geographical community connected through Internet access to participants in the global village.

Internet:
Global infrastructure of information and communication networks.

asynchronous threaded discussion:
An online forum for participants to communicate with a time delay.

The Benefits and Challenges of Online Writing

Leu and Kinzer (2000) report that teachers who use the Internet during the writing process enhance brainstorming sessions and the quality of peer editing through the exchange of digital drafts. For example, online writing labs or workshops provide students with feedback about their writing from assigned tutors or from participants of the intended audience prior to publication of the final product. In addition, Beach and Lundell (1998) used online communications to engage students in information exchanges in which students practiced how to present their beliefs and opinions on a controversial topic. Content analysis of these exchanges showed the online dialogue technique fostered reflection and development of language styles, which are important lessons for student writers to learn.

Online communications also pose unique challenges for teaching writing with middle-level students. Middle-level teachers are well aware that their students are psychologically vulnerable. At this time in students' lives, their personal identities begin to emerge along with their writing voices, which enables them to express their personal values, beliefs, likes, and dislikes. At no other stage in development are students more likely to encounter so many differences between themselves and others (NMSA, 2003b). Thus, students' online dialogue and peer critiques of one another's writing need to be monitored carefully. Rules of engagement can be set up to discourage bullying or other inappropriate interactions during written interactions among students. Adults in the online community are responsible for maintaining a positive learning environment and facilitating instructive feedback for budding writers.

Wallace (1999) explains that the Internet is often an identity laboratory, particularly appealing to young adolescents, who tend to be preoccupied with their developing self-images and personal writing voices for addressing authentic audiences as opposed to writing only for their teacher and a grade. They may try on different personas with a variety of perspectives before settling on one that fits with their emerging self. Teachers and writing mentors who use proximal instruction strategies foster students' metacognitive thinking, creativity, and personal voice, which are fundamental attributes of good writers.

Whether with a tutor, a peer, or a member of the prospective audience, online writing circles optimize the power and social value of interacting while learning to write. In the early days before networks, the computer had already proven to be an effective tool for facilitating writing instruction in learning environments, but the social characteristics of learning to write in an online community have added benefits. Donin, Bracewell, Frederiksen, and Dillinger (1992) were astute in recommending an approach to writing instruction that draws from the cultural context for the topic and requires the writer to address audience considerations when writing: "An important outcome of this research is the realization that writing must be treated simultaneously as a cognitive and social activity, and that these approaches, rather than being incompatible, are mutually reinforcing" (p. 210).

D'Agostino and Varone (1991) also emphasize the complexity of the educational task facing writing teachers and the fundamental value that social interaction plays in learning to write:

> Teacher intervention at the computer, where students have the ability to make immediate changes to their texts, can be powerful—perhaps even more powerful with some novice writers, who might be inclined to give up control of the text to the expert. In-process intervention, therefore, is a delicate and complex task that requires a skilled responder who is sensitive to the student's perception of the exchange, who helps students to improve their texts while preserving their individual voices. (p. 49)

More recently, researchers have noted that students must understand the context of an online writing situation in order to create a positive online relationship, particularly when they are asking for information or responding critically to another person's work (McNabb et al., 2002). This requires heightened audience awareness and attention to audience feedback. Teachers who use the Internet to facilitate writing circles explain that students also need to be aware of the difficulty in conveying emotions online and that they must be able to elaborate on an idea when asked for clarification from a peer or member of their intended audience.

When J.M. Wood (2000) reviewed published best practices for using technology in writing instruction, he found that the practices incorporated the writing process originally outlined by cognitive researchers (e.g., Flower & Hayes, 1980; Scardamalia & Bereiter, 1986). Many existing curriculum standards or frameworks for writing focus on the importance of students' writing processes. Prewriting is usually the first step in a writing assignment. During prewriting, the focus is on identifying the purpose of writing and what the audience needs or wants to know about a topic. Tapping students' initial thoughts in response to writing prompts or questions is an effective way to start the brainstorming process and to help focus students' thinking on a topic. Then teachers can stimulate students' thinking by asking them to generate their own questions to engage peers or guest experts in an online dialogue that exposes students to multiple perspectives and broadens their understanding of writing topics.

Teachers can use outlining or concept mapping techniques to assist students in organizing their ideas into an initial draft. Attention to narrative structure is important at this point in the writing process. Students also need to select a writing format for the text. Traditionally these formats include creative personal stories or a declarative, interrogative, exclamatory, or argumentative structure. In **networked classrooms**, students also write **hypertexts** with **interactive multimedia lexias** embedded into digital print. During drafting, opportunities to conduct information research on the Internet can help expand students' knowledge about the

networked classroom:
Environment in which students and teachers use the Internet for educational purposes.

hypertext:
Digital print with hyperlinks readers click on to access other texts.

interactive multimedia:
Related multimodal information that can be presented together with hyperlinks.

lexia:
A single block of narrative, images, sounds, or other media within a hypertext.

social context for their writing. After students have generated their initial drafts, they can benefit from constructive feedback and critiques. Reviewers should use specific evaluation criteria, methods, or protocols for responding to a draft with suggestions for improvement as well as their personal responses as readers. Online, this is an interactive process between the writer and the reviewer facilitated by online communications tools. The revision phase of writing can take many paths. Some drafts may need the flow of text reorganized, some may need elaboration on main points or illustration of subpoints, and some may need paragraph-level clarification. These are considered macrostructure revisions that change the overall conceptual meaning of a text. Microstructure revisions involve changes to word choices, text edits for transitional phases and sentence-level clarification, grammar, and spelling. When students author hypertext or interactive multimedia, writing becomes even more complicated as they have to choose between media formats and determine the purpose and structure of **hyperlinks**.

hyperlink:
Clickable text that connects to other hypertext or interactive multimedia.

Internet communication tools can converge with word processors and bibliography compilers that support digital print development with grammar, spelling, and style checkers and comment writing functions. Students also can use online dictionaries or thesauruses to expand their vocabulary and apply new words in the context of their own writing. Online, students also have opportunities for importing video, music, pictures, and diagrams into their writing. When designing the writing projects, teachers may want to consider places on the Internet where the students' work can be displayed and set up methods for readers to respond to the work within online learning communities. Taking this step in the writing process reinforces the value of writing to students, who are often eager to connect with peers and adults outside their immediate social sphere. Publishing online provides them with invaluable opportunities to learn about writing through open-ended reader responses and interactive dialogues with authentic readers.

From initial brainstorming to writing the first draft, reviewing and revising it, and publishing, the Internet provides an excellent forum for engaging middle-level students in interactive discourse and authentic audience response activities that can help them develop their personal voice and self-expression. The role of feedback in developing effective self-monitoring and revision strategies, which are the hallmarks of expert writers, can be greatly enhanced by engagement in online discourse and scaffolded writing activities with writing mentors in a distributive learning community. Internet tools such as instant messaging, synchronous chats, e-mail, and threaded discussions can be used for structured reader response forums, peer and mentor critiques of drafts, and audience response activities. To learn more about online resources to support writing instruction, visit the Web resources in Table 7.

TABLE 7
Online Writing Process Resources

http://web.mit.edu/writing/Writing_Process/writingprocess.html
Massachusetts Institute of Technology hosts an Online Writing and Communication Center with resources that explain and illustrate how to teach the writing process online.

www.nwrel.org/assessment/about.php?odelay=1&d=1
The Northwest Regional Educational Laboratory hosts resources about the 6+1 Trait Analytical Model, useful for assessing students' writing.

www.webenglishteacher.com/creative.html
Web English Teacher hosts a website full of exercises and ideas for teaching creative writing.

Internet Tip: Websites shift in content and location periodically. Although care has been taken to list reliable websites, sometimes sponsors change or move webpages without notice to their readers. To find additional resources on this topic, conduct a keyword search at www.google.com or use your favorite search engine.

Keywords to Consider: *writing process +online +writing circles*

Online writing instruction involving partnerships between university-based writing labs and K–12 students are emerging as a way to provide students with individualized feedback on their writing process because teachers typically do not have time to consult individually with students about their writing. Teachers also are partnering with local community organizations who train volunteer literacy tutors to act as writing tutors. A main goal of online writing instruction is to help students develop autonomy in their writing by scaffolding their development of self-assessment skills. These include critical reading about the purpose, audience, and organization of a draft (Beach & Lundell, 1998). Castleberg and Closser (2000) piloted the use of a university-based writing lab to enhance the feedback students receive about their writing. They found that effective tutoring strategies build rapport with student writers, use a reader response approach to posting comments, and foster student writers' skill at asking specific questions that elicit instructive feedback about their writing. Additional research shows that when students write with a Web-based place to publish and a real audience in mind, their motivation to work harder at developing and revising their writing increases (Brandjes, 1997; J.M. Wood, 2000).

The Harry Potter Online Writers' Workshop highlighted in this chapter shows how student writers in grades 4 through 6 participate from remote locations in a **collaborative learning environment** that aligns with the characteristics shown in Figure 7. The workshop immerses students in a social learning context for developing writing skills and knowledge, resulting in published work. During the workshop, students address many of the middle school English language arts standards

collaborative learning environment:
A password-protected workspace for groups.

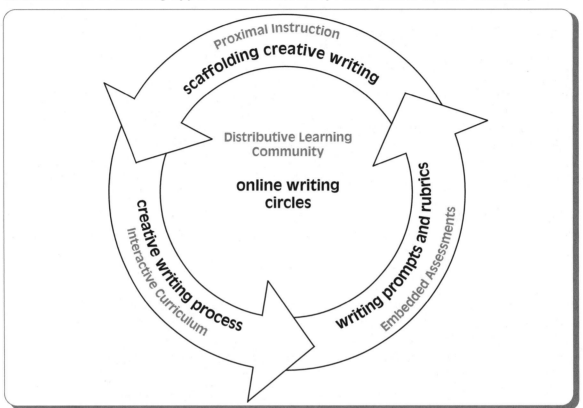

through their discussions of how characters, plot, and setting are developed. They take that understanding to a deeper level of personal knowledge by applying it in the stories they write. Students engage in peer-to-peer interactions in synchronous chats and intervene in one another's writing processes. For this reason, the teacher's role as a skilled reader and facilitator responding to students' drafts within the online writing circle is crucial. Online assignments can help students internalize revision strategies that are modeled among participants of the learning community. Requiring students to respond to constructive feedback and modeling the process of revision based on feedback shapes students' self-monitoring and revision strategies. The workshop described in this chapter uses print as the mode students use to communicate their ideas. However, the writing process also applies to authoring hypertext and interactive multimedia that can be published on a CD-ROM, DVD, or webpage.

The Harry Potter Online Writers' Workshop

Curriculum Objective: To scaffold students' development as writers by immersing them in the writing process within online writing circles.

Materials: *Harry Potter and the Order of the Phoenix* (Rowling, 2003); weekly access to the online writers' workshop via a password-protected collaborative learning environment.

Time Frame: 12 weeks

Technology Standards: Addresses the NETS-S (ISTE, 1999) under the categories technology productivity tools and technology communications tools.

Design of the Interactive Curriculum

The Online Writers' Workshop uses the Harry Potter series as the basis for discussing literary aspects of narrative fiction such as character and plot development. Students, who typically range in age from 9 to 12, read the book *Harry Potter and the Order of the Phoenix* (Rowling, 2003) as a model for their own creative writing. Throughout the workshop, they engage in online dialogue about J.K. Rowling's writing techniques and learn how to apply these techniques to writing their own stories. The workshop is offered by Northwestern University's Center for Talent Development as part of their distance learning program, Learning Links (see www.ctd.northwestern.edu), and hosted through the online Collaboratory (http://collaboratory.nunet.net). During the workshop, students discuss how elements of fiction, such as characters, plot, and setting, are developed. They take that understanding to a deeper level of personal knowledge by applying these elements to stories they write. The workshop also addresses grammar and editing, spelling, and punctuation. The students work on mastering the art of telling a good story through effective word choice and sentence and paragraph development. They use technology to produce compositions and multimedia texts while participating in the online learning community.

The format of the writing workshop includes online writing circles in which peers collaborate and teachers provide one-on-one mentoring throughout the writing process. Bonnie Thurber, known online as Mrs. T, coteaches the workshop with Carol Lee, the writing mentor, known as Mrs. L. Students complete the workshop with enhanced writing skills and original creative stories. To achieve that goal, students create **storyboards**, maintain **e-notebooks**, conduct online research when appropriate, and write multiple drafts of their stories. Students create at least one polished short story by the end of the 12 weeks. Written assignments are typically due on Mondays. Other assignments involve interacting with those in the online learning community and reviewing one another's drafts according to the schedule outlined in Table 8. Because the workshop is online, dialogue among

storyboard:
A writing technique used to organize notes.

e-notebook:
A password-protected online student journal.

TABLE 8
Online Writers' Workshop Curriculum Sequence

Sequence	Events
Week 1	Students are oriented to the online collaborative learning environment and workshop netiquette via a phone call from their teacher. Students, parents, and teachers collaboratively develop a schedule for the synchronous workshop events.
Week 2	Students introduce themselves in the workshop's threaded discussion forum and complete the 6 Ws survey.
Week 3	Students begin the prewriting and brainstorming process in their e-notebooks and participate in synchronous chats. The teachers use internal e-mail and the e-notebook Comments feature for private tutoring.
Week 4	Students focus on developing their characters and setting for their stories and participate in a threaded discussion and a synchronous chat session about this topic.
Weeks 5–6	Students build their story outline in their e-notebooks and read and discuss one another's e-notebooks during synchronous chats and asynchronous threaded discussions. Private coaching continues using the e-notebook Comments feature and internal e-mail.
Weeks 7–8	Students focus on writing storyboards to combine setting, characters, and plot outlines from their e-notebooks. When ready, they write a first draft with attention to word choice and story structure and engage in an asynchronous threaded discussion about these techniques.
Weeks 9–11	Students engage in various rounds of revision supported by synchronous chats and threaded discussions to ask and answer clarifying questions that focus their writing on answering the 6 Ws. Teachers coach individual students using the e-notebook Comments feature for private tutoring. When a story draft is ready, one of the teachers copies the narrative into a word-processing document and uses the track changes tool to model editing strategies for students to review. Students complete the story rubric for their own story and one another's stories. Each student reviews editing suggestions and responds to them in his or her e-notebook. Teachers select excerpts from students' e-notebooks to share with the entire group to model the revision process during synchronous chat sessions.
Week 12	Students share their polished stories with one another and with parents during the online symposium. Students are required to read and write a reader response for at least two stories written by their peers. Parents and students also participate in a synchronous chat to discuss the stories. Parents use the story rubric to provide students with personalized reader responses.

participants takes place in several modes and assignments are weekly rather than daily. Students engage in synchronous chats, exchange internal e-mail messages, participate in asynchronous threaded discussion forums, and use the Comment function in the e-notebook workspace for collaboration. In asynchronous collaboration, the student works online and then goes offline. Later, the teacher reviews the work online, comments on it, and goes offline. The student then returns at a convenient time to read and respond to the teacher's comments. Students also interact asynchronously. Although students are required to spend 1.5 hours a week on workshop activities, most students become so involved that they spend twice that much time or more on workshop activities.

The workshop begins with students dividing their e-notebooks into five parts that represent the stages of story writing: (1) prewriting/brainstorming, (2) character development, (3) outline/plot development, (4) storyboard development, and (5) working draft. Each student has an e-notebook that stores the student's work in a place where other students and the teachers can review it and post comments in response. Students access support materials for their writing online during the workshop. (Some of the Web resources for the workshop are listed in Table 9.) Once the student stories are complete, their work is published in an online gallery, with parental permission, and an **online symposium** is hosted by the Collaboratory with invited guests who are encouraged to read and respond to the students' work. Students retain all ownership rights to their stories.

online symposium: A gathering of invited guests showcasing student work and eliciting reader responses.

Bonnie and Carol encourage the students to integrate elements of other genres, such as poetry and nonfiction research and writing, into their stories when relevant. For example, a student may need to research a cultural setting for a particular scene or write poetic prose to describe a particular character. Students also have the opportunity to petition to work on a genre other than fiction, although writing Harry Potter episodes intrigues most of them. Bonnie and Carol regularly respond to students' e-mails and comment on all student work posted in each student's e-notebook. In addition, Bonnie and Carol are available online and via telephone to consult with parents and students, as necessary.

TABLE 9
Harry Potter Online Writers' Workshop Websites

www.bbc.co.uk/schools/revisewise/english/writing
The ReviseWise English website, hosted by the British Broadcasting Corporation, includes materials focused on story writing.

www.hp-lexicon.org
The Harry Potter Lexicon is an unofficial website hosted by Harry Potter fans and used by students and teachers alike as an encyclopedia to keep track of the numerous Harry Potter details.

www.glencoe.com/sec/writerschoice/parentsite/index_awm.html
The Glencoe Online Writer's Choice website, sponsored by publisher Glencoe/McGraw-Hill, links to numerous resources for teaching reading and writing in the middle grades.

Organizing the Distributive Learning Community

The students who participated in the workshop discussed in this chapter resided in six states across the United States, except for one U.S. student who lived in China. Typically students in the workshop come from all regions of the United States and never meet face to face. Therefore, it is imperative that Bonnie and Carol establish friendly methods for collaboration and interaction. The workshop's collaborative learning environment lends itself to students' exploring their own and their peers' ideas. They often feel freed by the Internet to express themselves in ways that they may not do in nonnetworked classrooms. Online, they do not fear speaking in front of the group, for example. They push themselves to participate because their contributions are visible and acknowledged by the learning community. Early in the workshop, Bonnie and Carol present a short lesson on **netiquette** to help students establish norms for their online collaboration. Netiquette, which is discussed in more depth in chapter 2, guides online behavior and provides a method for teachers to manage interactions online. During this lesson, students learn that they are expected to abide by the rules of engagement shown in Table 10.

In addition, students log in to the collaborative learning environment with assigned nicknames or first names only to protect their individual privacy. Students

netiquette:
Online communication etiquette.

TABLE 10
Netiquette for Online Writing Circles

Netiquette Rules of Engagement
- Behave as you would at school or at home.
- Be courteous, respectful, and helpful to others in this learning community.
- Clearly identify yourself and use your official nickname or log-in name at all times when posting dialogue or comments online.
- Do not criticize spelling or grammar as long as they are correct enough to understand the author's meaning. Strive to use complete sentences, real words, and proper printed language, but keep in mind that while working on the Internet, particularly in fast-moving synchronous chats, students and teachers may use language shortcuts familiar to the learning community. If you see a language shortcut that is unfamiliar, you should ask, "What do you mean by _____?"
- Make sure all the work you upload or post is your own. Students are to respect the copyrights of posted files and comments of others. You may not upload or make available files to which you do not have legal access.
- Be responsible for your individual account in the collaborative learning environment and take reasonable precautions to keep others from using your log-in name and password.
- Use appropriate language and do not use profane, vulgar, rude, threatening, or disrespectful language or personally attack other users.
- Keep the learning community dialogue focused on writing theme-based short stories and meet elsewhere online for other conversations or purposes.

are expected to make a positive contribution to the artistic climate in the online writing circles and to be polite and show respect for others whose perspectives may differ from their own. All writing for the workshop is available for review by the students' parents or guardians at any time. Teachers have a legal obligation to report any online writing that implies or depicts potential harm to students themselves or to others and to share suspect writing with the director of the program and with the student's parents immediately. Only those registered for the workshop and their parents or guardians can access the workshop, which is held in a password-protected environment online.

Assessment Embedded to Support Reflection and Revision

During the first week, students complete an online survey called the 6 Ws, in which they respond to the questions in Table 11. Bonnie and Carol use the information from the survey as a diagnostic assessment of students' prior knowledge about elements of fiction and story writing. After taking the survey, students can view the results for everyone in the learning community and discuss the survey with other students via a scheduled synchronous chat. This exercise starts students critiquing what they have read while giving them insight into how other students interpret the Harry Potter books. Bonnie and Carol scaffold the online dialogue that follows the survey to prompt students to start writing from an author's viewpoint.

TABLE 11
6 Ws of Story Writing

1. WHAT is the title of your favorite Harry Potter book?

2. WHO are the main characters in that book?

3. WHAT is the basic conflict in that book?

4. WHERE does the story take place in that book? There may be several settings for the story, so try to include all of them.

5. WHEN do you imagine the action in that Harry Potter book took place? Please explain how you came to your conclusion.

6. HOW was the conflict resolved in this story and WHY do you think J.K. Rowling handled the conflict in that particular way?

Your own short story will need to address these same Who, What, Where, When, Why, and How questions called the 6 Ws. Are you familiar with these 6 Ws?

      O Yes and thanks for reminding me about the 6 Ws.
      O No, I do not know about the 6 Ws.

Bonnie and Carol embed assessment into the story writing process by familiarizing students with the Story Rubric for Student Writers (see page 91) and referring to its criteria often throughout the workshop. Students use the story rubric to self-evaluate the strengths and weaknesses of their own stories and to make revision decisions about their drafts. The rubric focuses on character development, plot, structure, and writing elements (e.g., spelling, grammar, word choice). Students reinforce their learning by applying the rubric criteria to make observations about one another's writing and to provide instructive feedback during synchronous chat sessions and when embedding review comments directly into one another's developing drafts. Bonnie and Carol take advantage of the unique opportunities in the collaborative learning environment to model how experienced writers review and revise their writing to focus their viewpoint and audience awareness.

Bonnie and Carol also give students a set of guiding questions for each phase of the writing process and use the questions to promote students' self-reflection while writing (see Table 12). The guiding questions serve as self-assessment prompts after the online learning community uses them to critique and discuss the Harry Potter text. Students also apply the questions to critique and review the work of their peers. For their final assessment activity, students are required to read

TABLE 12
Guiding Assessment Questions

Prewriting and Brainstorming Questions
- Have I included interesting and rich descriptions and details that go beyond the obvious or predictable?
- Have I shown what was happening, rather than telling, using sensory cues in creating this story—so the reader can see, feel, smell, hear what I feel?
- Have I described my characters so the reader can visualize them?

Drafting Questions
- Have I grabbed the reader's interest from the beginning?
- Is my story readable and does it flow?
- Do the details I've included support the story, rather than distract from it?
- Does every scene add something to accomplish my purpose for this story?

Revision Questions
- Have I maintained a clear point of view and tone in my story?
- Will my voice lead my reader to see the story as I intend—but still have room for their own imagination to be active?
- Is there enough change of scene to hold the reader's attention but not so much that the story is lost?
- Have I chosen the words that will convey my meaning exactly and avoided confusing my reader?
- In my ending, did I leave my reader with something to think about?

STORY RUBRIC FOR STUDENT WRITERS

Title of the Story:

Student Author's Name:

Reviewer's Name:

Rating Scale: NW = Needs Work; G = Good; VG = Very Good; E = Extraordinary

Creative Story Critique Criteria	Reviewer's Rating
The story's first sentence or paragraph captures the reader's attention and the reader cannot help but continue reading.	
The problem or conflict in the story is clear. It is fresh and new.	
The author shows what is happening, rather than telling the reader.	
The story's characters and settings are described in enough detail so that the reader can visualize them.	
The descriptions and details are very rich and interesting; they go beyond the obvious or predictable.	
The author uses sensory cues in this story—so that the reader can see, feel, smell, and hear what is happening.	
There is enough change of scenery to hold the reader's attention, but not so much that the reader gets lost or confused by the story.	
In the ending, the reader is left with something to think about.	

Please write a paragraph below to describe your thoughts and feelings about the story right after you finished reading it.

All of us have grown as writers, and mainly because we have encouraged one another along the way! Please write to the author below to tell him or her what you liked most about this story.

Literacy Learning in Networked Classrooms: Using the Internet With Middle-Level Students by Mary L. McNabb with Bonnie B. Thurber, Balazs Dibuz, Pamela A. McDermott, and Carol Ann Lee. Copyright © 2006 by the International Reading Association. May be copied for classroom use.

and reflect on two stories written by their peers. As part of the peer evaluation process, they write a paragraph that describes the thoughts and feelings they have about the story after they finish reading it.

Applying Principles of Proximal Instruction

During the workshop, Bonnie and Carol work as a team to model positive, constructive feedback and questioning strategies within the online writing circles. They also use a variety of instructional strategies to support each student in his or her unique zone of proximal development. These include modeling writing tasks during one-on-one and small-group dialogue sessions, analyzing drafts and proposing customized revision tasks, and probing students to self-monitor their responses to instructive feedback. The collaborative learning environment allows Bonnie and Carol to coach individual students to learn the techniques of story writing and to encourage students on a personalized basis as they organize their ideas in a coherent story narrative. Bonnie and Carol routinely monitor students' online interactions and occasionally find a student posting an inappropriate comment. In these instances, Bonnie or Carol will use internal e-mail messaging to coach the student privately in ways to rewrite his or her comments so the feedback is instructive rather than offensive to peers. Students learn to value collaboration with their peers and the multiple perspectives they can glean from it to shape their audience awareness and understanding of the social context for their writing. The following sections highlight the work in progress of one student, Dee, to illustrate how the teachers scaffold students' development as writers. All the students in the workshop receive similar attention.

Brainstorming Story Topics. Once students have introduced themselves and are familiar with how to collaborate online, the action quickly moves to brainstorming their story ideas in their e-notebooks. They also engage in prewriting activities during synchronous chat sessions, which expose students to one another's differing perspectives and broaden their understanding of potential writing topics. The following excerpt from Dee's e-notebook shows how she began creating the characters for her Harry Potter episode. Bonnie and Carol reviewed and responded by embedding suggestions in her e-notebook.

Dee's E-notebook

Tupa—New student who is really nice, joins the quidditch team, and is best friends with Harry. She likes to wear tulips in her long, red, shiny hair. Reminds kids of Fluer Delacour. Instead of silver hair, she has red hair! She has an accent. It's hard to hear what she's trying to say sometimes. She is a clever witch like Hermione, but less bossy.

Mr. Aurnt—Mr. Weasly's new boss. Likes to lay around, bossing people around. Almost never showers, (disgusting!) and a lot of people avoid him. Flies find a place to live now. (With Mr. Aurnt)

Shy Mig—Shy Mig is Hermione's new owl. She is a brown owl with small white spots all over her body. She is really shy and likes to stay around Harry so Hermione and Harry switch owls.

Kyle Clack—Brown dark hair, new star of the Quidditch team. Is the new beater. He is in fourth year. He used to go to Dumstrang with Krum. Hermione starts going out with him.

Mark Sack—Geeky, nerdy, wears glasses, carries a kLnex with him everywhere. Is the exact opposite of Kyle Clack.

Teacher Comments

These are good for one-line descriptions. Take some time and write a bit more. Make me "smell" the characters with your words!
Mrs. T

I'm not so sure I'd like to "really" smell these characters, but Mrs. T is right. They are strong characters who surely have their own unique (ugh) smells, strange habits, and such.

I love the idea of V....being a house-elf, even though that probably keeps people fooled, and I guess I'd want them to be able to defend themselves against him (rather than being fooled and then hurt).

Here's an idea to help you fill out more details about your characters. Read several pages of HARRY POTTER and notice how much is packed into many of the sentences. Rowling draws a picture with sounds, movements, expressions, and words. Try this out by adding some of these details to what you have written here about these characters.
Mrs. L

Throughout the semester, Bonnie and Carol monitor the students' e-notebooks and embed comments such as these to help each student build confidence in his or her writing and at the same time point out a train of thought that might be developed further. Students know that as they continue to write, their teachers will be reading and writing feedback to assist them in developing their stories. As participants of the online writing circles, students also have the opportunity to review and respond to one another's e-notebooks. This online access allows students to learn from how their peers complete the various assignments in the writing process. When they read a peer's e-notebook, students are required to use the guiding assessment questions (see Table 12 on page 90) to structure their comments in one another's e-notebooks, which the student writer then responds to during the next round of writing or in scheduled synchronous chat sessions.

The weekly synchronous chat sessions facilitate dialogue among participants of online writing circles as they respond to one another's work. Chat transcripts are saved so students and teachers alike can download the dialogue for later retrieval. Bonnie and Carol discovered through experience that when students review and reflect on these transcripts, it helps them begin to organize their outlines and notes into storyboards and a first draft. The following is an edited transcript from a synchronous chat in which Carol mentored Dee as a means of demonstrating for all the students how to develop a story outline. This chat transcript retains the time-stamp to show how rapidly the **posts** take place. Posts are labeled A, B, C, etc., to show the parallel conversations that occurred during this chat session. Carol simultaneously facilitated the discussion about Dee's outline and responded to Alison, who arrived late to the chat and could only see posts from that time forward. The chat window only displays a certain number of posts due to its memory capacity, and so as participants post new comments at the bottom of the window, earlier comments disappear at the top. Carol also followed up on a few new topics introduced by students. The rapid ebb and flow of topics is one of the hallmarks of chats that teachers need experience facilitating in order to become skilled.

post:
A message submitted during online dialogue.

A [19:50] Rahul: Why does the new house elf throw ron's glove into the lake

B [19:50] Alison: what did I miss?

B [19:50] * Danielle waves

A [19:50] Dee: because he's trying to get Ron to go to the lake

A [19:50] Jessie: oh, because i think that if you put it into a story, it would really be exciting

A [19:50] Dee: ok

B [19:50] Danielle: Well this chat is ending in ten minutes and we are looking at Dee's outline

A [19:50] MrsL: Dee, from the comments, it sounds like the same thing would be helpful here as for the other outlines... Some details that answer the questions we have

B [19:51] MrsL: Ali we are discussing Dee's outline

A [19:51] Dee: Tupa overhears that Keazel puts Ron's gloves in the Lake

C [19:51] Rahul: What do they get for Christmas?

C [19:51] Dee: yea, a favorite teacher

B [19:51] Alison: ok

B   [19:51]   Jessie: oh

C   [19:51]   Dee: Ron gets the gloves for Christmas

C   [19:52]   MrsL: regular gloves?

B   [19:52]   Danielle: 7 students are here

D   [19:52]   Jessie: what's so special about them

D   [19:52]   Rahul: Harry and Hermione?

D   [19:52]   Dee: they are Ron's favorite team

E   [19:53]   MrsL: any more ideas for Dee...questions?

E   [19:53]   Dee: i'm ready for more

E   [19:53]   MrsL: she's ready, definitely...she's done lots of writing

E   [19:53]   Jessie: great outline

E   [19:54]   Alison: i dont think i have any more questions

E   [19:54]   Rahul: really good

E   [19:54]   Dee: thanks

As the brainstorming process continued, students began organizing their ideas into outlines. Students are encouraged to think about and organize their plots in a series of scenes that identify the major actions and important places for their characters. They are required to fill in important details within each scene, using a letter or number system. Because all the students have a unique take on their stories, they are not required to follow a strict outline format, only to have the elements within each scene carefully ordered and with enough detail to make the outline clear to the teachers and the other students who will be discussing the outlines in the weekly chat session. The following sample from Dee's outline illustrates the process.

Dee's E-notebook

I. Chapter 1—Goodbye Dobby
    scene a. Dobby dies, leaving Harry Potter no help.
    scene b. Harry Potter has a dream about Dobby dying.
    scene c. Dobby was murdered.

II. Chapter 2—Changes at Hogwarts
    scene a. Snape becomes the Defense Against the Dark Arts teacher.
    scene b. A new student comes to Hogwarts.
    1. Her name is Tupa.
    2. She is really nice to Harry.

3. She's in Gryffindor.
scene c. Firenze becomes the Potions Teacher.

In the following excerpt from another synchronous chat session, Carol used Dee's outline as a model to scaffold other students' thinking about how they would outline their story scenes. This transcript was edited to focus attention on a single conversation within the group.

Mrs L: Dee, can we look again at your outline to give Sonam an idea how chapters work together?

Dee: sure

Mrs L: Ok, let's go to Dee's e-notebook

Alison: i'm there

Mrs L: you're fast!

Sonam: i'm there

MrsL: tell us what happens after the duel?

Alison: what's the ending

Dee: well, if the dueling is the last chapter, then we wouldn't have something to like describe what happened to them

Mrs L: I C . . . Have you thought of an ending yet?

Dee: they're going to duel, then Harry, ROn, and Hermione become friends again

Sonam: kool

Mrs L: Sonam, do you see how Dee is telling her story, step by step, in her outline?

Sonam: yes

While Carol encouraged the students to read and discuss one another's outlines, other students logged in and started to catch on as they began to discuss how their stories would end. Carol assigned students whose learning had accelerated to act as writing mentors to help other students organize their notes into story scenes. Students could move easily between one another's e-notebooks and a synchronous chat session to read one another's work and then discuss it during the drafting phase of the writing process. When students are able to conceptualize their stories scene by scene, they are then ready for the next step, which is generating a first draft.

Generating Drafts. During the workshop, students learn to generate story drafts by arranging their notes and outlines into sequential storyboards organized around a main plot and related supporting ideas. During this phase of the writing process, Bonnie and Carol review the students' e-notebooks and begin coaching them about how to write about the plot from the scene outlines and notes they generated during the brainstorming activities. Students may opt to use concept mapping or an expanded outline to organize their storyboards. Attention to narrative structure is important at this point in the writing process. Students also need to select a writing format for the text, such as creative personal stories or a declarative, interrogative, exclamatory, or argumentative structure. At this point, opportunities to conduct information research on the Internet can help expand students' understanding of their topic or the context for their story. While generating storyboards, students in the workshop are prompted to use the guiding assessment questions (see Table 12 on page 90) for self-reflection and when reviewing one another's storyboards. Students begin sharing their scenes when they are ready. The following is an excerpt from Dee's e-notebook about the setting for one of her scenes.

Dee's E-notebook—Setting

Scene b—Privet Drive
Harry lays in his bed at Private Drive at night. He tries to fall asLp as he listens to the loud banging of the trashcans on the smooth street. As he finally drifts off, everything stopped. It is quiet. A loud voice breaks the silence. A cold, harsh voice. "Tell me about Harry Potter or else," the voice threatens. A scream filled the air. "No! I will never give any secrets about the great Harry Potter." "Very well," the voice continued as the sound of a chair spinning echoed the room. "Avada Kedavra," he whispered. A green, blinding, light filled the room. Harry awoke with a start. That was the end of his dream. Cold Sweat glides down Harry's face. He could almost taste the sweat. His ears were ringing in silence. He could see nothing but pure darkness.

Teacher Comments

I really enjoyed reading this! It is taking a very nice shape. I have taken the time to suggest how to divide it up into paragraphs. Please look at the embedded comments in your e-notebook :)
    There are some ideas...that you can probably rewrite that will make this flow a bit better. Some of your sentences need to have more in them. Break up the dialogue like I suggest in the paragraph. Remember, each new speaker needs a new paragraph.
Mrs. T

Bonnie posted these comments as a private message to Dee, who would see them the next time she logged in to the collaborative learning environment. This example illustrates one of the unique ways teachers can use the Internet to interact with students about the discipline of writing while immersing the student in his or her own writing process. Peers also learn how to post review comments to other students, which reinforces their understanding of the writing techniques they are learning. The personalized review and response activity provides student writers with an understanding of how well they are communicating their ideas to an audience and prepares them for making meaningful revisions.

Making Meaningful Revisions. Knowing that revision skills develop through experience, Bonnie and Carol scaffold students' opportunities to revise with assignments that ask them to reflect upon and respond to feedback from others in the online learning community. They also help students make decisions about what—and where within a draft—revisions need to be made. In the following excerpt from a synchronous chat, Bonnie used a questioning strategy to stimulate students' thinking about revision techniques. Again, this transcript was edited to focus attention on a single conversation within the group.

MrsT: i have a q

Dee: fire away

MrsT: what happens in Hogwarts Castle-kitchens that makes the story end the way it does...why is that scene important to the story?

Dee: well, we have to meet Keazel for the story to happen that way

MrsT: yes, so we meet him...but what is in him that makes the story happen that way?

Dee: we need to know him to get suspicious

Alison: why do we have to meet Keazel in the 3rd chapter?

MrsT: ok...so, how can you weave stuff around him to make us all suspicious? why the kitchen and not somewhere else? what is special about him in the kitchen.

Dee: Well, he's a house elf he works in the kitchen

* MrsT nods...why is he in the kitchen at this point in the story...

Dee: Well, we need to find out about him

MrsT: ok...what do you need to find out?

Alison: doesn't dobby work in the kitchens?

Dee: no he died

Alison: oh yea

Dee: he used to though

Alison: ok

MrsT: is that something you want to include?

Alison: so maybe you could have keazel take dobbys place in the kitchens?

Dee: yea

* MrsT smiles. Ok

As students come closer to finishing their stories, they post a complete draft so that everyone in their writing circle can give feedback to help fine-tune the stories for publication. At this point, Bonnie and Carol model how editing even the smallest detail is important in preparing a story for its readers. Attention is given to careful word choice and cohesive story structure. Students learn that good writers spend a great deal of time editing their work. At the same time, students learn to focus on the overall narrative structure and logic of the story they are telling.

Student Showcase

The workshop culminates with students completing their original short stories and publishing these online in the workshop gallery, which is accessible to invited guests as well as students during an online symposium. The polished stories are due one week before the end of the workshop to allow teachers time to post the student work for the online symposium, which takes place on the official end date for the workshop. The finished stories represent extended tales of the Harry Potter characters as well as the introduction of new characters, settings, and dilemmas to solve. Bonnie and Carol conduct the online symposium for parents and other interested family members who are encouraged to take part in a synchronous chat with the workshop writers as well as to provide feedback using the story rubric. During the online symposium, readers and writers discuss the students' original creative stories, share praise, and evaluate the overall workshop format. The following excerpt from the online symposium displays a portion of Dee's story and a reflective comment about her writing from an invited guest.

Chapter Nine: The Quidditch Theft, by Dee
The next day, Harry walks back from History of Magic. It is the last class of the day and everyone is tired. Harry slumps into a comfy, purple chair near the fireplace. He has lots of homework. He starts by reading a book on Famous Spell Inventors. As he reads, something small sneaks by. It looks like a blur of tan. It sneaks up to the boy's dormitory where Ron is sleeping. As Harry follows it, he ends up near Ron's trunk.

"Who's there, and why are you going through Ron's stuff?" Harry wonders out loud.

The elf's head turns around. Its eyes are filled with surprise.

"Harry Potter! What a surprise. I wasn't expecting you here," Keazel the elf stammers.

"This is where I sleep," Harry says. "What are you doing here, and why are you looking through Ron's clothes?"

Keazel pauses. "It is my job to keep the castle clean. Please excuse me and continue with your reading," Keazel continues rummaging.

"Do you need help Keazel? If you tell me what you're looking for, or what you're trying to clean, I will try to help," Harry says.

Keazel shakes his head.

Harry nods and sits in his bed reading his History of Magic book. One eye focuses on the words, and one eye is watching Keazel closely. After about an hour, Keazel stops what he was doing.

"My job here is done, Mr. Potter. I hope I have not disturbed you. Good night, Harry Potter," Keazel grunts. He stalks off.

Parent Comment

I especially enjoyed the creative variety of verbs and adjectives used to describe the characters' emotions. The author did a fantastic job of creating realistic and interesting dialogue between characters. The conversations flow naturally and it is easy for the reader to see/hear them taking place. Great job!

The value of the collaborative learning environment shows in students' final stories and their ability to reflect on the work of their peers and to communicate their reactions responsibly. Teachers who carefully scaffold students' interactions and assignments during online workshops can create a truly distributive learning community that intervenes effectively in students' writing processes to foster their development as writers.

Conclusion

The effectiveness of collaborative learning environments, such as the one described in this chapter, often depends on how teachers structure interactive assignments to keep students engaged in participating with others across time and space. Clocks no longer define the moment in which learning takes place within online distributive learning communities. School walls and geographical locations no longer define student groupings. In the ideal classroom, each student would receive a significant amount of guidance from a writing mentor, but in reality this does not often happen because teachers do not have the time and tools to give personalized guidance. Online writing workshops, however, provide a community of learners who can receive guidance and mentoring from teachers as well as each other. Middle-level literacy learners need interactive practice with the writing process to hone their self-expression and academic discourse skills. As they continue through the writing process, they become increasingly responsible for requesting and accepting feedback not only from their teachers but also from one another and for responding with quality revisions.

This chapter illustrates how to use the Internet to sustain the activities of a writers' workshop, which provides students, teachers, and writing mentors with opportunities to intervene in one another's writing as audience members, as colearners, and as participants of a literacy community. These are value-added benefits of using the Internet for writing instruction. Chapter 6 describes a four-step process to guide readers in designing their networked classrooms to provide students with effective literacy learning opportunities.

GUIDING QUESTIONS FOR DISCUSSION

1. What are some techniques useful for designing the curriculum and sequence of activities for an online writers' workshop?

2. How can teachers assess students' cognitive, social, and basic technology readiness abilities—that is, students' readiness to participate in online writing and publishing activities?

3. What social norms and monitoring strategies are suitable for governing students' participation in online writing circles?

4. How can teachers embed assessment into their students' online writing process? How can assessment criteria be enforced online?

CHAPTER 6

Designing Networked Classrooms

networked classroom:
Environment in which students and teachers use the Internet for educational purposes.

Internet:
Global infrastructure of information and communication networks.

global village:
Networked cultures around the world connected via the Internet.

collaborative learning environment:
A password-protected workspace for groups.

World Wide Web:
Public portion of the Internet's online information resources.

I have had the privilege of observing many teaching practices in **networked classrooms** while working as a program evaluator for technology-related school improvement initiatives. Through interviews with teachers, I often find those who are new to the networked classroom harbor many professional development concerns related to their beliefs and attitudes toward the **Internet** that tend to parallel the types of practice I observe in their classrooms. Teachers who have acquired learner-centered strategies for managing students' use of highly interactive curricula and embedded assessments affirm that the Internet is a welcome addition to the literacy learning environment. Others, less familiar with the pedagogy of networked classrooms (discussed in chapter 2), often experience chaos at first.

For teachers who are novices in the networked classroom, it is best to ease into connecting the classroom with the **global village**. Teachers can start by designing lessons based on a familiar curriculum method, for example. All three units described in chapters 3, 4, and 5 adapted methods from nonnetworked classrooms. The Huck Finn's Journey unit in chapter 3 incorporated use of a **collaborative learning environment** to extend literature circles and information research activities that started in the nonnetworked classroom. For those students, the Internet enriched their ability to comprehend historical fiction and its real-life context. In the Understanding Human Body Systems unit in chapter 4, the **World Wide Web** was incorporated as one among many information research resources. Those students learned how to locate and evaluate digital information online and to select sources appropriate to a larger inquiry project involving a problem-solving curriculum method. The Harry Potter Online Writers' Workshop described in chapter 5 portrays a more extensive use of a collaborative learning environment in the sense that the online workshop *was* the classroom. Nonetheless, students involved in the workshop engaged in an established writing process methodology. In addition, all three units in chapters 3 through 5 incorporate printed books.

Fostering students' pleasure in reading print is important. Print can teach students about linear narratives. Narratives tell stories about the world in coherent ways. Print authors often take great strides to explain their story sequence or narrative logic. They purposefully avoid overwhelming or disorienting their readers. In contrast, online **hypertext** and **interactive multimedia** contain **multisequential** text structures, which often present readers with a diverse array of reading options accessible through clicking on **hyperlinks**, often in places that require students to filter out incoherent or disparate ideas. However valuable print will continue to be, the social context for literacy increasingly requires use of the Internet for personal, professional, and academic purposes in **networked cultures**.

The Four-Step Design Process

This chapter provides an overview of how to design learning opportunities that empower students to meet the new literacy challenges found in networked cultures. The suggestions are meant to further challenge teachers who have an understanding of how to adapt existing curriculum and pedagogical practices when starting to use the Internet in networked classrooms. The resources and examples in this chapter illustrate ways to transform the English language arts curriculum while addressing student diversity, taking advantage of **virtual communities**, and using digital assessment tools. Emphasis is given to pedagogical strategies that tap the power of distributive learning communities and help teachers pull it all together. This chapter explains the following four-step design process to guide teachers' use of the Design Template for Networked Classrooms (see page 104):

Step 1: Design an interactive curriculum that incorporates the Internet's digital information and communication resources in ways aligned with 21st-century literacy and technology learning standards.

Step 2: Organize the various teaching–learning roles and norms within the distributive learning community to fit the instructional methods in the curriculum design.

Step 3: Create benchmarks for using technology to embed assessments into students' online learning activities to measure their developmental progress on an individual and group basis.

Step 4: Plan proximal instruction strategies for scaffolding the diversity in students' literacy performance in developmentally appropriate ways.

Step 1: Designing an Interactive Curriculum

It behooves teachers to think strategically about when and how the Internet will enhance their literacy curriculum because access to networked classrooms is costly and

---

hypertext:
Digital print with hyperlinks readers click on to access other texts.

interactive multimedia:
Related multimodal information that can be presented together with hyperlinks.

multisequential:
Allows for diverse reading options in a single hypertext.

hyperlink:
Clickable text that connects to other hypertext or interactive multimedia.

networked culture:
A geographical community connected through Internet access to participants in the global village.

virtual communities:
Groups whose members are connected through Internet access for a specific purpose or common interest.

DESIGN TEMPLATE FOR NETWORKED CLASSROOMS

Interactive Curriculum Design

Student literacy learning needs:

Curriculum objectives:

Online digital resources:

Distributive Learning Community Plan

Teaching–learning roles:

Rules of engagement and netiquette guidelines:

External learning partners:

Embedded Assessment Plan

Benchmark checkpoints:

Assessment resources and digital tools:

Guided assessment practice sessions:

Proximal Instruction Plan

Student observation schedule:

Proximal instruction strategies:

Accommodations for diversity:

---

oftentimes limited. The best use of scarce resources is to design the curriculum in ways that give students learning experiences that are otherwise inaccessible. McNabb and colleagues (2002) report that most teachers interviewed in their study began using the Internet to access a wider array of curriculum resources and current informational text not found in textbooks. In addition, teachers cited the benefits of collaborating through online dialogue and sharing documents with other teachers and students in the global village as motivating factors for using the Internet. Teachers who use the Internet attest that it enables students to perform at high levels of literacy, induces them to write more fluently, fosters keen audience awareness, and challenges them to develop critical reading skills. In the study conducted by McNabb and colleagues, teachers demonstrated a variety of ways to guide students on a personalized basis during online curriculum assignments. For example, experienced teachers who work in networked classrooms routinely created an index of options for students and asked them to choose one to master. They found that students often are savvy enough to recognize which option best fits their instructional needs even when the options are not labeled developmentally. These teachers also actively monitored students' online literacy actions, which provided ample opportunities to observe how students' literacy development differs.

When designing the curriculum, teachers should keep in mind the following tips:

- Review students' literacy progress in relationship to English language arts and technology standards to identify the range of learning needs among students.

- Define the series of curriculum objectives aligned with standards that students will achieve while engaging in a particular digital curriculum unit or lesson.

- Conduct online research to review educational indexes and directories, which are useful guides for selecting digital resources that can support students' literacy development.

Aligning Objectives With Learning Needs. For teachers, the Internet offers opportunities to design lessons that are adaptive to meet the needs of students at various levels of literacy development. Online, students typically engage in reading and writing activities that deepen their comprehension and self-expression beyond that of a print-based curriculum alone. An interactive literacy curriculum, supported through the Internet, can align with many of the standards for the English language arts (IRA & National Council of Teachers of English, 1996), especially the following:

- Conducting research on issues and interests by generating ideas and questions, and by posing problems.

- Gathering, evaluating, and synthesizing data from a variety of sources (e.g., print and nonprint texts, artifacts, people) to communicate their discoveries in ways that suit their purposes and audience.

- Adjusting use of written and visual language (e.g., conventions, style, vocabulary) and employing a wide range of writing strategies to communicate effectively with a variety of audiences and for different purposes.

computer network:
Computers connected by communication lines.

- Using a variety of technological and informational resources (e.g., libraries, databases, **computer networks**, video) to gather and synthesize information and to create and communicate knowledge.

- Developing an understanding of and respect for diversity in language use, patterns, and dialects across cultures, ethnic groups, geographic regions, and social roles.

- Participating as knowledgeable, reflective, creative, and critical members of a variety of literacy communities. (p. 3)

These English language arts standards overlap with the NETS-S (ISTE, 1999) for students' use of productivity, communication, and research tools and for students' development of positive attitudes toward using the Internet to support their learning, collaboration, and personal pursuits.

Standards are broadly stated curriculum goals meant to guide the development of curriculum objectives for literacy learning at various levels. In the United States, the national English language arts standards and technology standards have been developed by separate entities. Thus, curriculum committees and teachers have the task of articulating objectives that integrate technology into the content area curriculum in ways that foster students' development of technology skills in service of reading, writing, and information research learning. Table 13 describes sample objectives for a proposed curriculum unit design for developing students' ownership of literacy in the global village.

Once objectives for the appropriate curriculum standards are defined, teachers locate and evaluate Internet-based resources that can scaffold students' litera-

TABLE 13
Sample Curriculum Objectives

Students will increase their ownership of literacy by

- Accessing an assigned WebQuest with supportive texts that help them comprehend a series of trade books within a cultural unit of study.

- Engaging in online dialogue about the trade books and online reading of supportive texts with an assigned literacy mentor to enhance their comprehension and vocabulary.

- Producing a blog to express their interpretation of the trade books and their cultural context.

- Monitoring reader responses to their blogs and interacting with members of their virtual community through structured blogging sessions.

cy learning. The types of online resources will vary depending upon the focus of the learning experience. The sample objectives in this chapter require access to a collaborative learning environment that can host online interactions among virtual community participants as well as provide links to the **blogosphere**. Individual lessons included in the proposed unit can focus students' online reading using curriculum designs with structured hyperlinks to **supportive texts** that enable students to create their own reading paths. Teachers either can join existing virtual communities whose projects address current curriculum objectives or consider designing their own virtual community project using an **open source** collaborative learning environment. Table 14 lists some online resources compiled to help guide teachers' online curriculum research.

blogosphere:
The collective virtual community of blog writers, readers, and texts.

supportive text:
Print enhanced with hyperlinks to text or interactive multimedia.

open source:
Software code and online applications for free download.

TABLE 14
Online Curriculum Design Resources

www.ipl.org/div/blogs
The Internet Public Library hosts a blog where teachers can learn more about how to connect students to the blogosphere.

www.webquest.org
The official WebQuest homepage provides a starting place for those interested in designing an inquiry-based online reading experience for students.

www.Moodle.com
This open source application enables teachers to create their own collaborative learning environment for use in networked classrooms.

www.teaching.com/keypals
The KeyPals Club is a useful resource for teachers interested in joining existing virtual community projects with participants from diverse regions of the global village.

www.quia.com/jg/66106.html
A Feast of Homonyms makes learning new words fun for students while helping them become better independent readers and online information researchers.

www.lexiteria.com/translation
The Lexiteria offers online translation services for foreign languages including foreign vocabulary words.

Internet Tip: Websites shift in content and locale periodically. Although care has been taken to list reliable websites, sometimes sponsors change or move webpages without notice to their readers. To find additional resources on this topic, conduct a keyword search at www.google.com or use your favorite search engine.

Keywords to Consider: Use terms in the glossary of this book as keywords in combination with terms about instruction methods such as literature circles, writing workshops, or information research.

Enriching the Curriculum With Digital Resources. Using digital resources, teachers can provide students with access to content that elaborates on topics of interest on a variety of reading levels. Students' natural curiosity may take them well beyond the assignment requirements. For those needing help, teachers can create supportive text webpages to link together audio, video, pictures, and print texts that illuminate the meaning of difficult-to-comprehend concepts. Designing a curriculum for the networked classroom also requires teachers to locate and evaluate websites for content, reading levels, authorship, and the context of hypertext links to and from other online information resources. Teachers may want to work with a librarian or media specialist to identify online information resources that can be grouped together in this manner.

An advantage of an interactive curriculum is its potential for providing students with critical reading and vocabulary development opportunities otherwise unavailable. Research shows the importance of middle-level students' continuing to build their vocabulary to increase comprehension (Blachowicz & Fisher, 2000; Cassidy & Cassidy, 2001/2002; Moore et al., 1999). Using the World Wide Web, when a student finds a new keyword in a **search return list** but cannot decode its meaning, the student can type "definition:keyword" into a **search engine** and readily acquire its dictionary definition. A student also can use synonyms and homonyms to help him or her comprehend key concepts and examine how others use new terms in a variety of contexts. In addition, the curriculum often challenges students to compare and contrast their own perspectives with the multiple perspectives of others. It encourages them to analyze complex ideas found in informational and multicultural texts and to practice taking ownership of their literacy in the global village.

search return list:
A collection of Web resources compiled by a search engine.

search engine:
An online program used to index and access the contents of registered websites.

Step 2: Organizing the Distributive Learning Community

Once teachers experience success and gain confidence teaching familiar lessons in their own networked classroom with their own students, they can expand their repertoire of curriculum designs to include a broader array of roles and invite external mentors and learning partners to participate in the online learning events. Doing so will maximize the benefits of the networked classroom for developing students' literacy skills that are applicable to the global village. Chapter 2 discussed in depth the dynamics of the teaching–learning cycle in effective networked classrooms, which call for a shift in roles within the learning community.

When organizing distributive learning communities, teachers should keep in mind the following tips:

netiquette:
Online communication etiquette.

- Identify the different roles for participants during the curricular activities.
- Establish rules of engagement and **netiquette** as guidelines for online collaboration and behavior expectations.

TABLE 15
Sample Teaching–Learning Roles

- Students select their own readings within the WebQuest and pose their own comprehension questions that guide the focus of online dialogue among themselves, their assigned literacy mentor, and blog participants.

- Teachers recruit and train external partners to use proximal instruction strategies to scaffold each student's comprehension of the trade books, WebQuest supportive texts, and blog reader responses.

- Literacy mentors share their cultural background knowledge to scaffold students' cultural exchanges with blog participants and to expand students' use of new vocabulary when interpreting readings.

- Teachers present and reinforce the criteria for writing the blogs, and the literacy mentors provide students with guidance in making decisions about the form and content of their blogs.

- Recruit and train external literacy mentors who will enhance students' learning opportunities, and collaborate with other teachers or experts in the global village.

The Second Information Technology in Education Study found common patterns for teaching–learning roles in networked classrooms in 28 countries (Kozma, 2003). For each student role, there was a corresponding teacher role. The student roles associated with information research involved working in pairs or as participants of a collaborative research team. These teams use digital information resources such as the Internet, CD-ROMs, spreadsheets, and databases to collect and analyze data related to solving a particular problem. The corresponding teacher role was to pose important research questions and draw out students' own research questions. Teachers also monitored students' information research and collaboration processes and explained important concepts or knowledge when necessary. In addition, teachers assisted in structuring students' research activity plans. Table 15 describes the teaching–learning roles appropriate to the proposed curriculum objectives in Table 13 (see page 106).

Establishing Rules of Engagement. The rules of engagement for a particular group depend to a certain degree on characteristics of the participants, for example their age, and learning objectives for the group. In contrast, netiquette is a more widely accepted set of norms governing online behaviors and use of language (see chapter 2 for more information on this topic). When designing rules of engagement for a particular distributive learning community, keep in mind the types of interactions inherent in the roles teachers and students play during the assignments. It is often helpful to review how others have used rules of engagement along with netiquette to establish the norms and expectations for online behavior among a group of students. The rules of engagement for each of the curriculum units in chapters 3–5 provide good examples. In addition, Tapscott (1998) set up the following rules of engagement to govern a group of adolescents involved in an online project called the Growing Up Digital Interactive Forum:

> You know the rules of Netiquette or else you wouldn't be here. It all comes down to the golden rule: "Treat other people as you would yourself be treated."
>
> You are entitled to express your opinion.
>
> You are entitled to an audience.
>
> You are expected to learn.
>
> You are expected to teach.
>
> You have a right to disagree.
>
> You have a right to respond.
>
> It is your privilege to change your mind.
>
> It is your privilege to remain silent. (p. 67)

It is important for teachers to set high expectations for participation online. Establishing online group norms, rules, and rights helps create a nurturing learning environment. In distributive learning communities, students learn to take personal responsibility for regulating their behavior according to a set of guidelines that are reinforced. When a student fails to abide by the rules, it is usually highly visible online, and teachers can swiftly address misbehaviors to maintain the cohesiveness of the group.

While literacy researchers place a great deal of importance on the value of the Internet as a vehicle for participation and exchange, teachers are more likely to have their students use the Internet for research and publishing than for participation in online collaboration and dialogue (McNabb et al., 2002). Participants in the McNabb and colleagues study reported that their institutional acceptable usage policies made it difficult to use the Internet for purposes of engaging students in virtual communities. In the study's survey, "participation in online discussions" and "e-mail correspondence" were the two Internet uses most likely to be disallowed by respondents' institutions. This may be due to concerns about quality control and safety issues. School administrators and governing boards need to work with teachers to resolve institutional barriers that hinder students' access to online learning opportunities. Policies that restrict curriculum design to information research and Web publishing prevent students from reaping the full benefits of their networked classrooms.

Collaborating With External Literacy Mentors. The communications capacity of the Internet enables external partnerships to serve various teaching–

learning roles within a distributive learning community. According to NMSA (2003a), teaming is an important characteristic of effective learning environments for young adolescents; however,

> the effectiveness of teaming is dependent on factors such as the frequency and amount of common planning time, number of students per team, the length of time or experience in teaming, and professional development [for teachers] focused on effective teaming practices. (p. 36)

In addition, George and Lounsbury (2000) hail the value of multiage groupings.

To take advantage of teaming, teachers can design online activities to include literacy mentors who assist students in completing their literacy assignments. Identifying and selecting literacy mentors can be a research project for teachers. Before inviting participants from outside the classroom to join students, teachers should establish the parameters and modes for interaction between external literacy mentors and students. For example, inviting college students to act as online writing mentors for young adolescents requires prescreening of the older students to ensure that their social ethics are mature enough for the task. External literacy mentors should receive training about netiquette and rules of engagement that include formal agreement about their roles.

Teachers can recruit members of the local community to serve as reading buddies as well. Reading buddy programs enlist members of senior citizen groups or volunteers from corporate sponsors to tutor struggling readers identified by local schools. Reading buddies work closely with students' teachers to review the strengths, weaknesses, and personality of students so that students are matched with appropriate buddies. Reading buddies can hold regularly scheduled online sessions with students to discuss what they are reading and to tutor them as needed. These types of arrangements involve long-term commitments and regular interactions among participants. Making a variety of dialogue modes available, such as **synchronous chats** and **asynchronous threaded discussions**, allows participants to adapt their schedules and avoid traveling to meet in person. When possible, schools may host kick-off meetings and ending celebrations face to face to further develop students' sense of community.

synchronous chat:
Real-time exchange of online dialogue between multiple participants.

asynchronous threaded discussion:
An online forum for participants to communicate with a time delay.

Other common partnership practices among Internet-savvy teachers include structured question-and-answer sessions between published authors and students, which typically involve a one-time online discussion, rather than ongoing literacy mentorship. Teachers often find it helpful to elicit student questions and convey these to authors before the discussion date. Students also can conduct interactive presentations with online audience participants. Teachers can organize parent organizations to participate in audience awareness events in which readers respond to student writings published online. It is helpful to provide audience participants with a common rubric to guide their reader response as Bonnie and Carol did in the unit in chapter 5. These strategies emerging in networked classrooms can extend learning opportunities for groups of students. Boundaries for online group membership can range from those who are within a particular school, to students in different schools, to intergenerational participants from around the global village. Online activities also can be set up for literacy clubs that may have operated as a group prior to becoming electronically networked. In these cases, the Internet enhances communication and resources for those in the club. It also makes flexible their time frames for participation.

Initially, students may not understand that others' perspectives can differ from their own, which is acceptable. However, they may need coaching in how to respond amicably to others without igniting **flame wars**. To accomplish this, teachers can invite local librarians, other area teachers, community members, and parents to participate in online activities and help bridge cross-cultural misunderstandings. In this way, online activities can provide students with a strong sense of community, which endures beyond specific online events. Taking this route gives students a chance to practice their netiquette and become comfortable taking personal responsibility for their online behaviors.

flame war:
A sequence of hostile messages exchanged online.

Step 3: Planning for Embedded Assessments

Once the objectives and associated roles are identified, the next step involves planning assessments that easily can generate data about learners' developing literacy during a lesson or unit. Classroom-based assessments are embedded into students' learning activities so that teachers can monitor their learning and gather data on which to base instructional decisions. Embedded assessments do not carry high-stakes consequences and are generally challenging and motivating to students. Assessments that identify students' instructional needs, rather than ranking students according to a norm, help students understand themselves as learners.

When planning embedded assessments, teachers should keep in mind the following tips:

- Identify checkpoints for measuring students' literacy development and design observable benchmarks for each checkpoint.

- Select assessment resources and digital tools that can be embedded easily into learning activities and generate quick and useful data aligned with benchmarks.

- Provide students with guided practice using technology-supported assessment tools, including practice using different testing formats and interpreting technology-generated feedback.

Findings from the study conducted by McNabb and colleagues (2002) indicate that the most prominent ways participating teachers embedded assessments into students' online learning involved measuring students' ability to read informational text accurately, compare and contrast information sources, synthesize multiple sources on a topic, and organize information into a personally meaningful structure. Teachers also noted the value of assessing the depth of the information students obtain online, their ability to meet deadlines, and their ability to reflect on their literacy development in a journal. Teachers can collect reader responses to student work from an authentic audience and then require students to consider the feedback while reviewing and revising their work.

Identifying Checkpoints for Assessment. Planning embedded assessments starts with articulating checkpoints at the critical junctures in literacy development and then designing assessment benchmarks that describe expected student performance and how and when it will be measured during the lesson or unit. Benchmarks should align with objectives established for the unit, which in turn align with district, state, and national standards. For example, the benchmarks described in Table 16 are suitable checkpoints for the curriculum objectives in Table 13 (see page 106).

Classroom-based assessments embedded into students' learning are a cornerstone of effective networked classrooms. These types of assessments generate data that enable teachers to observe and respond quickly to students' learning processes through instructional feedback. According to Wiggins (1993), effective assessment feedback compares a student's performance with an exemplary benchmark and indicates consequences of good and poor performance. Productive feedback also supplies back-up resources and guidance to help the student troubleshoot problems that may impede his or her future performance.

TABLE 16
Sample Benchmarks for Curriculum Objectives

- Teachers monitor students' reading daily through online dialogue retellings.

- Teachers provide content and miscue analysis with written feedback to the students about the level of their comprehension in the daily online dialogue archives.

- Literacy mentors analyze and provide written feedback about the appropriateness and scope of new vocabulary word usage in the students' blogs.

- Literacy mentors analyze and provide written feedback about the students' literal and figurative comprehension of the trade books and supportive text in the blogs.

- Teachers review and provide feedback about students' written reflections based on structured reader responses from those participating in the blog.

Cumulative research from the learning sciences has led to a deeper understanding of the important role of feedback from assessments embedded in the learning process. Effective classroom-based assessments are part of the interactive curriculum and generate data that benefit both teachers and students (see, e.g., Bransford et al., 1999; Chung & O'Neil, 1997; Pellegrino, Chudowsky, & Glaser, 2001) by

- identifying the diversity in students' prior knowledge, which serves as the basis for tailoring instruction;

- acknowledging and building on the range of students' achievement levels;

- recognizing students' misconceptions or gaps in their knowledge that instruction can address; and

- stimulating students' future learning by engaging and motivating them in deeper levels of analysis on a personalized basis.

Bransford and colleagues (1999) indicate that "the key principles of assessment are that they should provide opportunities for feedback and revision and that what is assessed must be congruent with one's learning goals" (p. 128). In effective networked classrooms, teachers scaffold the development of students' self-assessment habits and metacognitive skills for reflecting and acting on assessment results. Analysis and feedback are important aspects of effective teaching (McAninch, 1993). Assessments that provide students with practice responding to feedback about their literacy abilities help them develop metacognitive self-assessment skills that will serve them as lifelong literacy learners. Increasingly, more digital assessment tools are becoming available for the networked classroom for these purposes.

Selecting Assessment Resources. Regular use of digital assessment tools tends to shift teachers' time away from data gathering to an emphasis on data analysis and designing follow-up interventions. Tools such as literacy portfolios can warehouse formative data and make the data Web accessible in hypertext or interactive multimedia formats for students, parents, and teachers to review. In addition, educators and computer scientists have been working on developing digital assessment tools to facilitate scoring of open-ended responses such as essays (Burstein, Marcu, Andreyev, & Chodorow, 2001; Foltz, Gilliam, & Kendall, 2000; Kintsch, Steinhart, Stahl, & LSA Research Group, 2000). These tools allow students to analyze their own drafts by automating essay grading. Students can then immediately respond to the feedback by making appropriate revisions and rerun the assessment to see how they have improved. The digital assessment tools use sophisticated pattern-matching procedures as the basis for scoring. Surprisingly, research shows these tools score at rates comparable to scores generated by teachers. Nonetheless, students need to be prepared at a level of literacy that enables them to detect and dismiss mistakes in automated feedback when it occurs due to the limitations of computers to process natural human language. They need to understand both the benefits and the limitations of all the different types of automated grading applications they encounter in order to avoid following erroneous advice on the screen.

Even the readability tools embedded into word-processing applications are useful for self-assessing writing. For example, the Flesch–Kincaid Grade Level Index and the Flesch Reading Ease Score will automatically analyze a text document in Microsoft Word according to standard grade-level criteria. The index computes readability based on the average number of words per sentence and average number of syllables per word. The readability score is displayed in terms of grade level. For instance, a score of 7.0 means the text was written at the seventh-grade reading level. Teachers can use this information as a quick assessment of a student's writing level and group students accordingly. By cutting and pasting text from a webpage into a Word document, teachers can easily evaluate its reading level to determine whether or not it will be a useful curriculum resource for students at a particular reading level. Teachers also can post Socratic questions in asynchronous threaded discussion forums and capture students' written responses with a time stamp, which indicates how efficiently each student is able to respond. Because online communication tools enable all students to respond, written dialogue can be used as a method of formative assessment about every student's thinking, which is not possible in a verbal discussion.

Student response systems (for face-to-face settings) can quickly deliver multiple-choice questions to students. These types of applications allow teachers to set parameters for how data are displayed on **interactive whiteboards** (e.g., according to individual performance, subgroup performance, or whole-class performance). The systems also include the option of setting a timer for the purpose of motivating students to pay attention. Teachers who use these systems memorize students' numbers and instantly recognize who is and is not participating or responding correctly. Students respond using a **handheld remote** that electronically logs each student's answer according to the number on the interactive whiteboard. Students know to watch for their response to appear on the whiteboard and tend to be more attentive in these networked classrooms. Once time runs out, it is easy to display aggregated results in graphs or charts that show students how they are performing. Online test applications can be used in a similar way with students responding via a computer keyboard. Teachers can then engage in proximal instruction lessons that provide students with immediate feedback about their answers. Teachers can use these systems to conduct quick comprehension or vocabulary quizzes and to adapt lessons instantly to address common misconceptions or to reinforce learning by building on students' observable achievements. Students who have access to these types of learning

student response system:
A system used for question-and-answer interactions between teachers and students.

interactive whiteboard:
A wall-mounted projection screen with touch sensors that control a computer.

handheld remote:
A portable device used to send wireless signals from a user to a computer.

opportunities tend to gain awareness not only of their literacy achievements but also of their unique learning styles and developmental needs. They start taking responsibility for monitoring their literacy learning based on guidance from timely and useful assessment feedback.

Step 4: Planning Proximal Instruction Strategies

The purpose of proximal instruction is to scaffold students' literacy development within the context of their literacy learning processes. Proximal instruction strategies foster students' ability to perform at increasingly higher levels of independent reading and writing. Teachers who practice proximal instruction adapt their teaching in response to students' literacy performance, which they routinely observe and monitor. Teachers use a variety of scaffolding strategies during proximal instruction (McNabb, 1996; for more detail see chapter 2).

When planning for proximal instruction, teachers should put emphasis on accommodating student diversity, keeping in mind the following tips:

- Develop a schedule for monitoring each student's unique literacy learning processes during online activities.
- Identify a variety of strategies to scaffold specific aspects of the curriculum as appropriate for the differences among the students involved.
- Monitor and scaffold collaboration among members of the learning community to support students' literacy development.

Teachers can rely on the interactivity of the curriculum and timeliness of embedded assessments to help them understand each student's unique learning processes and areas requiring instructional intervention. The natural variance among students in the middle grades is amplified in the networked classroom. Hypertext readers who have not yet developed their internal narrator, for example, often become disoriented by the lack of cohesive narratives online. Likewise, student writers who have weak self-monitoring skills may allow immediate audience feedback to disrupt their focus and lose sight of their personal purpose for communicating. Important aspects of students' learning processes may have been unobservable in the nonnetworked classroom, in which students are often receivers of lessons rather than doers of literacy acts.

In addition, the hypertext and interactive multimedia features of the World Wide Web have the potential to act as teaching aids to assist students in acquiring new literacy skills. Teachers can create webpages with hypertext links that bridge print reading with companion readings online to expand students' opportunities for comprehension. Online readings also can explain how literature relates to real-world contexts to enhance students' meaning making. Table 17 presents some strategies suitable for the proposed activities outlined in Tables 13, 15, and 16.

TABLE 17
Sample Proximal Instruction Plans

- Teachers negotiate collaborations among online literacy mentors, students, and reader response participants for the student blogs.
- Teachers assign the modes of online dialogue suitable for each student.
- Literacy mentors assist students in setting benchmark goals for comprehension fluency and interpretation of readings presented in their blogs.
- Teachers model for literacy mentors how to elicit reflective thought and interpretative analysis from students with regard to assigned readings.

Scaffolding Online Reading. Teachers are fortunate that the Internet makes it possible for them to observe how well students are monitoring their reading choices. By conducting routine observations of individual students while they are reading online, teachers can observe aspects of students' reading processes in action. Specifically, teachers can watch for

- what students click on and their sequence for reading,
- how long they stay with a particular **lexia** on the screen,
- their body language, and
- their distractibility or level of persistence.

lexia:
A single block of narrative, images, sounds, or other media within a hypertext.

Behaviors such as mouse use (e.g., scrolling and linking) and use of online tools such as search engines and the **Find command** also are indicators of how well students monitor their comprehension.

Students who struggle to monitor their own comprehension of hypertext can benefit from guided practice sessions focused on developing comprehension fluency. For example, if a teacher suspects a student is having trouble reading hypertext, he can prepare a small collection of webpages and observe the student's online reading behavior for five minutes and gather data about each lexia of hypertext and the sequence the student uses to navigate through the text. After the teacher notes how long the student spends on each lexia, he then can ask the student to retell verbally or in writing what she read. If the student cannot develop a cohesive narrative that describes logical connections between lexias in the hypertext she accessed, most likely she is not monitoring her reading choices carefully enough to comprehend hypertext.

Find command:
A Web browser tool used to search a page for a word or phrase.

Scaffolding reading in the networked classroom means prompting students to explain their rationale for clicking on certain links when their reading process appears chaotic. This approach can help students internalize a questioning strategy for monitoring their reading decisions and resulting comprehension. Having students keep an annotated hyperlink **log** requires that they reflect on and articulate their reasons for constructing their narrative path within a hypertext. The log acts as a reading record with telltale signs about the level of comprehension the student has achieved.

Teachers can design discussion questions to prompt students to summarize their hypertext reading and **hypertext link path**, predict future research findings, or express beliefs and feelings related to what they read. Online discussion transcripts, whether from a synchronous chat or an asynchronous threaded discussion, can be preserved so that teachers can review and analyze every student's level and quality of participation. To assist students with developing their comprehension, teachers also can provide instruction about text structures used in print genres and compare how these structures may or may not apply to information on the World Wide Web. Teachers can use a projector and ask students to verbalize their thinking as the group previews the headers, connective links, and other text organizers on the Web. As teachers gain experience in the networked classroom, they will be able to develop a repertoire of strategies for scaffolding students' reading experiences.

Scaffolding Online Information Research. Teachers can address learner differences associated with online research by requiring students to document what they focus on while researching. Capturing students' electronic search histories, for example, provides a source of information for students to refer to while they explain their reading logic. Most students benefit from assignments that require them to focus on key aspects of the information research problem or question. They also can plan search sequences in small increments using a small number of keywords for each search session. Teachers can ask students to set research goals and map their progress toward their goals as a way to foster self-regulation for learners who require organizational support.

Research preparation activities that draw from students' prior knowledge can activate personal memory structures and enhance chances for students to acquire new knowledge online. For students who struggle with attention or memory problems, research subtasks should be small enough to complete within a 10-minute session. It may be helpful to encourage these students to use the Bookmark function in the **browser** toolbar to save links to websites they have found for later retrieval and evaluation.

Other organizational tasks can help students follow through on their research purpose. Students can learn to take real-time notes about what they read and to write annotated citations for informational hypertext pertinent to their research

log:
An automated record of Internet activity.

hypertext link path:
A reader's clickable text sequence through hypertext or interactive multimedia.

browser:
An online interface used to access and read hypertext and interactive multimedia housed on the World Wide Web.

topic. They can plan next steps based on a webpage they have read or set goals for what they need to find next to fulfill their research purpose. Teachers can use these techniques with students to help accommodate attention and memory weaknesses during online information research.

As stated previously, hypertext and the overall open-ended nature of the World Wide Web pose for all students literacy challenges that teachers can address with a variety of assignment options. Students who struggle with monitoring their comprehension do not make conscious reading choices in hypertext and may benefit from interacting with a literacy mentor who models self-monitoring strategies for synthesizing information across webpages. Most students also benefit from structured vocabulary building assignments that focus their awareness on comprehending new words they encounter in informational texts. With adequate scaffolding, all students can benefit from using the Internet for information research.

Scaffolding Online Writing. The act of publishing student work online provides students with authentic authoring experiences and tends to motivate young writers to do their best writing throughout the unit. Selecting the appropriate publishing forum is a valuable lesson for students as well. When designing writing assignments, teachers may want to consider places on the Internet where the students' work can be displayed and then set up methods for readers to respond to the work within a **blog**. Doing so reinforces the value of writing to middle-level students, who are often eager to connect with peers and adults outside their immediate social sphere. Publishing online provides them with opportunities to learn about the writing process through open-ended reader responses and interactive dialogues with authentic readers.

> **blog:**
> A Web log with dated entries that functions as an online journal.

Instructional techniques that facilitate development of a student's cognitive writing processes typically chunk writing assignments into manageable subtasks. The communication networks on the Internet can be used to support writing subtasks. In contrast to synchronous chats, asynchronous threaded discussions allow students more time to read and reflect before composing, editing, and posting their comments for others to see. In this online communication mode, teachers can outline discussion topics in a sequence to provide organizational cues to help students focus their attention on subtasks or important topics. Overall, threaded discussions tend to foster more reflective writing than chats or **instant messaging**. Teachers can organize an online discussion in an asynchronous forum that provides a time lag between **posts** for small groups of students who need more production time. This strategy gives students time to reflect on and revise their writing before posting it to the discussion forum for others to read. Writing mentors can further scaffold students' writing production processes through instant messaging prompts or queries to help them brainstorm responses during online writing events.

> **instant messaging:**
> One-on-one online dialogue in real time.
>
> **post:**
> A message submitted during online dialogue.

Students can use word-processing tools to compose their discussion comments or drafts before posting them. Students who struggle with writing at the microstructure level of text production can benefit from using grammar, spelling, and style checkers as editing aids. Those who struggle with writing at the macrostructure level of text production can be assisted by a writing mentor who replies to drafts with specific suggestions for improvement. Teachers can insert color-coded comments directly into students' drafts or make an alternative version of a draft and demonstrate organizational writing techniques using a student's actual text. These types of proximal instruction strategies provide scaffolding for students who struggle with producing written language.

In a group of students, the range of differences that appear during online writing activities may surprise teachers. These differences are due to the cognitive demands generated by audience interactions during the writing process and the nature of various online dialogue tools (for details see chapter 2). Rose and Meyer (2002) explain that decisions about how to use different types of media to accommodate individual learner differences can either support or hinder students' learning. Teachers who venture into cyberspace grow accustomed to recognizing and accommodating students' various developmental needs related to their reading and writing processes rather than simply grading the product of those processes.

Conclusion

A key aspect of integrating the Internet into middle-level classrooms is not choosing print over digital or digital over print curricula. Rather it is about deciding what resources will support students in acquiring the literacy knowledge and skill they need to succeed academically. It is about connecting the literacy curriculum to personal lives and to the networked cultures in which students live. It also means valuing print narratives as a way to show students how authors make connections so that the students understand how to make meaningful connections between lexias they read online. In addition, it is about supporting students as they find their voices and express themselves in the global village. Teachers who recognize the value of the Internet provide students with access to multiple perspectives, new vocabulary, interactive multimedia formats, and audience analysis opportunities that may only be possible online. In this regard, the Internet has a powerful role to play in the development of students' ownership of literacy. Students in the middle grades often differ enormously with regard to their rate of development overall. Some lag behind the expectation that they can read and write independently while others are on target or far more advanced. As students in the middle grades move through early adolescence at varying rates, teachers typically find them meeting expectations along a continuum of literacy development. For networked classrooms, teachers can plan curriculum, assessments, and pedagogical strategies that address diversity and allow each student to become fully engaged in learning. Chapter 7 provides a brief look at pressing concerns and trends facing literacy educators as they venture to do this.

GUIDING QUESTIONS FOR DISCUSSION

1. How does integrating the Internet into the classroom enable students to engage in literacy opportunities unavailable in the nonnetworked classroom?

2. How do embedded assessment tools help identify learning differences among students with regard to achieving literacy benchmarks?

3. What roles and guidelines support collaboration among teachers, students, and external literacy mentors within a distributive learning community?

4. Where in the literacy curriculum is the Internet most useful for preparing students to be literate citizens in the global village?

Trends Influencing the Future of Literacy Education

Many of today's middle-level classrooms were designed to prepare students with the literacy skills needed in nonnetworked cultures of the 20th century. Since the infusion of rapidly evolving information and communications technology networks across the globe, policymakers and educational leaders have been crusading for classrooms to move beyond industrial-age teaching–learning methods and curriculum materials to adopt practices for preparing young adolescents to live, work, and learn in the **global village**. Today's young adolescents will grow up to be global citizens competing for jobs in the world marketplace with the most highly skilled and highly motivated workers from other countries, and need new literacy skills to succeed.

global village:
Networked cultures around the world connected via the Internet.

Impact of Global Forces on Literacy

In the not-so-distant past, the majority of citizens, even in developed countries, did not require reading and writing skills beyond the eighth grade (Murnane & Levy, 1996). As a result, the focus in schools was on early literacy development involving simple comprehension tasks, a canon of common vocabulary, and familiar print text structures. However, teaching children the basics of reading and writing for print is no longer enough. The literacy demands in **networked cultures** go well beyond those of nonnetworked cultures. For example, Riel (2000) states,

networked culture:
A geographical community connected through Internet access to participants in the global village.

> Educational goals are tied to learning environments, as one changes so must the other. Literacy goals 100 years ago for many students were to be able to read and write names, copy and read texts, and generate lists of merchandise. Literacy goals of today require mastery over many different genres of writing, persuasive, expressive, expository, procedural [texts] and expect students to be able to interpret, compare, contrast, and analyze complex [digital] texts. (¶ 1)

In contrast, recent research shows that many adolescents have not developed their literacy beyond these basics, a trend that is severely limiting their opportunities to succeed in the global village (Kamil, 2003; Rasinski et al., 2005; Sen et al., 2005). Research consistently indicates that students may master primary reading and writing skills and fail to progress in their literacy development to keep fluent as they move through educational systems beyond fourth grade (Kamil, 2003; Sen et al., 2005). Literacy learning is a continuous developmental endeavor, and students in networked cultures face more literacy learning demands than any other generation due to the complexity of literacy acts inherent in uses of information and communications technology.

A consistent series of reports indicates that high school students in the United States are falling behind high school students in other developed countries because of their weak reading performances beyond the fourth grade (Donahue, Voelkl, Campbell, & Mazzeo, 1999; Kamil, 2003; Sen et al., 2005). Sen and colleagues report how the U.S. education system compares to other major industrialized countries (i.e., Canada, France, Germany, Italy, Japan, Russian Federation, United Kingdom) in reading. Their findings stem from multiple sources including international studies comparing educational reading achievement and students' attitudes toward reading in these industrialized countries. Fourth graders in the United States rank second in reading achievement; however, 15-year-olds in the United States are outperformed in reading by all seven of the other countries, even though U.S. students have significantly more access to remedial reading specialists and remedial services than students in these other countries (Sen et al., 2005). In addition, U.S. fourth graders show significantly lower levels of reading enjoyment and reading engagement than students of the same age in the other seven developed countries, indicating a correlation between pleasure in reading and reading achievement in the middle grades. These findings highlight the importance of fostering students' ownership of literacy. The **Internet** is an engaging literacy learning environment teachers can tap into to motivate students to participate in meaningful literacy activities.

The amount of time students spending reading in the middle grades is a factor in their overall achievement in schooling according to Paul (1996). In addition, the types of texts students read in the middle grades shift from stories that have highly structured narratives with clear and logical story plots, characters, and beginnings and endings to more complex informational texts in content areas. Furthermore, the texts found in **networked classrooms** can be very different from middle-level books. These texts contain **hypertext** and **interactive multimedia** structures that are **multisequential**. The **lexia** options embedded into online hypertexts remove any chance for hypertext readers to comprehend without critically reading and forming their own synthesis and conclusions. These are skills that appear on the higher end of the literacy continuum.

Internet:
Global infrastructure of information and communication networks.

networked classroom:
Environment in which students and teachers use the Internet for educational purposes.

hypertext:
Digital print with hyperlinks readers click on to access other texts.

interactive multimedia:
Related multimodal information that can be presented together with hyperlinks.

multisequential:
Allows for diverse reading options in a single hypertext.

lexia:
A single block of narrative, images, sounds, or other media within a hypertext.

Comprehension and fluency with complex texts are significant indicators of secondary students' overall academic achievement, according to research conducted by Rasinski and colleagues (2005). Bill Gates (2005) attributes the poor performance in young adolescents' reading performance, at least in part, to the need for schools to step up their efforts to prepare today's students for living and working in tomorrow's global village. He points out that students are not being prepared for the literacy challenges they face in high school and beyond. Schools need to do more to prepare them professionally to be knowledge workers. Teachers in the middle grades can address this dilemma by personally engaging students in literacy acts that involve reading, writing, and researching information via the Internet.

A recent global study that investigated the use of information and communication technology in the educational systems of 23 countries confirms that the Internet has become a positive force in the educational arena. It has the power to transform teaching and learning practices as well as profoundly influence the skills students will need to succeed in the emerging global village (Kozma, 2003). Many nations now recognize an increase in functional literacy demands. These demands are spurred on, in part, by the widespread influence of the Internet. The global movement among developed countries is to create educational accountability and assessment policies to govern use of the Internet in schools. Countries are responding by creating national curricula with literacy benchmarks and associated assessment mandates (Leu, 2000). Ireland, for example, established a National Reading Initiative at the same time it began an initiative to infuse information technologies into its schools. Australia, Canada, England, Finland, and India are among the countries launching similar efforts to prepare their youth to succeed in globally networked cultures and economies.

The United States has responded to this challenge with the No Child Left Behind Act of 2001 (NCLB; 2002). NCLB considerably raises the bar for academic achievement of all students and includes mandates for technology literacy for eighth graders and effective practices for using technology in teaching. While educational leaders, researchers, and policymakers debate the intricacies of NCLB and similar laws and policies in other developed countries, the long-term outlook suggests that the academic expectations for students will only increase due to global economic and technology trends.

When I reflect on visits to networked classrooms in which I have witnessed how the Internet can enrich literacy opportunities for students, I also am reminded of those on the other side of the digital divide. The stark difference between literacy activities in nonnetworked and networked classrooms was never more apparent to me than when I visited poor classrooms in India. In a rural jungle area, I saw modest campuses in the midst of tribal hamlets and overcrowded classes of up to 100 students per teacher. In Mumbia, a large urban city in India, classes were just as full. Some of the students went home to sleep amid the noise of busy streets. Most of the students were first-generation literacy learners and disadvantaged economically. Books were scarce in these classrooms. Students recorded their teacher's lecture notes from the chalkboard or verbal lessons on erasable tablets and committed to memory the lessons for the day.

In contrast, students in effective networked classrooms read and write in ways that foster autonomous expression and ownership of literacy. They analyze, synthesize, and generate knowledge as they read hypertext. They have opportunities to publish their work for others in the global village to read and respond. They can interact with experts and peers throughout the globe through various modes of online dialogue. They develop new vocabulary and literacy habits that shape their understandings of self and value within and beyond their geographical communities.

The open-ended nature of the Internet allows middle-level students to satisfy their natural curiosity about the world and their need for strong, supportive relationships in the context of academic undertakings. They can engage in **real-time** assessments that mirror their achievements and provide useful and timely feedback that informs their understanding of themselves as learners and serves as the basis for their teachers' decisions about how to adapt instruction to meet each student's unique learning needs. With the growing prominence of the Internet, inaccessibility to it for literacy opportunities only serves to deepen the digital divide. It is no longer an option but a necessity for students to learn to engage in the literacy discourse of networked cultures. This requires that they learn literacy online.

real time:
Live interactions online such as in synchronous chats.

Shifting Definitions of Literacy

Literacy instruction needs to keep pace with the social and cultural contexts for reading and writing in networked cultures. The middle grades are the place to meet these challenges by focusing on teaching students strategies for increasing their academic vocabulary, critical reading, and information research skills as well as encouraging their enjoyment of and engagement with literature. Effective instructional strategies and curriculum designs for using the Internet can boost students' literacy development beyond the basics. Teachers can begin transforming literacy learning opportunities in their classrooms by connecting traditional academic literacy with the new literacies of the 21st century. The Internet is rapidly changing the knowledge and skills people need to be literate in networked cultures. At the same time, students need to be competent in the traditional literacy skills applicable to print. The literacy demands for those living, working, and learning in networked cultures has increased well beyond the needs found in nonnetworked cultures. Teachers are obligated to provide students with scaffolded opportunities to learn a full spectrum of literacies found in the networked cultures in which they live.

Online texts have unique hypertextual and interactive multimedia characteristics that make them fundamentally different from conventional print texts. As a result, reading and writing within an interactive curriculum have fundamental differences compared to the literacy skills needed to succeed in the print-based curriculum. These differences and the cognitive demands they place on literacy learners are illustrated throughout this book. These are some of the new literacies. Leu (2001) points out that technology is changing the definition of literacy so rapidly in networked cultures that the process of becoming literate is now ongoing. Literacy learning is a lifelong challenge, which creates both new opportunities and new challenges for literacy educators. Leu writes,

> If literacy is deictic, and I believe it is, then the central question for each of us is not "How do we teach children to be literate?" Instead, the central question is "How do we teach children to continuously become literate?" That is, "How do we help children learn to learn the new literacies that will continuously emerge?" (¶ 3)

Young adolescents who are growing up in networked cultures are exposed to and often immersed in the vernacular of Internet pop culture. This means they routinely use **chat acronyms** and **emoticons** while reading and writing online. While these symbol systems are considered slang by some, others recognize their potential for becoming part of the language of the global village. Classrooms that are not networked to the global village are failing to bridge students' vernacular language with academic language. Although online language has not yet progressed to the level of its own established grammar, syntax, and genres, there are indications that it may.

Furthermore, young adolescents are growing up in networked cultures that rely on digital tools that are designed to make their daily tasks more efficient. However, these are not always the outcomes of technology. For example, students need to be made aware of how to use feedback from digital tools to aid their literacy development. Digital feedback is automated from many digital tools students in networked cultures encounter on a daily basis: Spelling checkers, grammar checkers, speech to text and online text translation tools, essay graders, and **search engines** all produce feedback that affects literacy. These automated tools do not perform flawlessly because they cannot comprehend natural human language, but they do allow teachers and students to narrow the probability for identifying and addressing mistakes. Although automated tools are not perfect, teachers can guide students in using them effectively. Without an awareness of the limitations of digital tools for processing natural human language, even the simple spelling checker can be viewed as a menace to literacy learning, as the poem by Jerrold H. Zar illustrates:

Candidate for a Pullet Surprise

I have a spelling checker.
It came with my PC.

chat acronym:
Slang used in online dialogue to save keystrokes.

emoticon:
A group of keyboard characters used to express emotion.

search engine:
An online program used to index and access the contents of registered websites.

It plane lee marks four my revue
Miss steaks aye can knot sea.

Eye ran this poem threw it,
Your sure reel glad two no.
Its vary polished in it's weigh.
My checker tolled me sew.

A checker is a bless sing,
It freeze yew lodes of thyme.
It helps me right awl stiles two reed,
And aides me when aye rime.

Each frays come posed up on my screen
Eye trussed too bee a joule.
The checker pours o'er every word
To cheque sum spelling rule.

Bee fore a veiling checkers
Hour spelling mite decline,
And if we're lacks oar have a laps,
We wood bee maid too wine.

Butt now bee cause my spelling
Is checked with such grate flare,
Their are know faults with in my cite,
Of nun eye am a wear.

Now spelling does knot phase me,
It does knot bring a tier.
My pay purrs awl due glad den
With wrapped words fare as hear.

To rite with care is quite a feet
Of witch won should bee proud,
And wee mussed dew the best wee can,
Sew flaws are knot aloud.

Sow ewe can sea why aye dew prays
Such soft wear four pea seas,
And why eye brake in two averse
Buy righting want too pleas.

(Reprinted with permission from the *Journal of Irreproducible Results*, January/February 1994, p. 13, www.jir.com.)

The poem demonstrates the limitation of digital tools, such as the spelling checker, for processing natural human language by showing how automated information processing functions. The computer-generated language mistakes in Zar's poem illustrate how computers do not comprehend the differences between homonyms, for example. For literacy teachers, this can be a hazard, but for students not well versed in the intricacies of the English language, the mistakes may go unnoticed. After all, readers do understand the gist of the poem's message despite its unconventional grammar and spelling. If we compare a poem written in today's standard English to one written in standard Middle English, we might see similar grammar and spelling differences. Technology is rapidly shifting the English language, and teachers need to keep abreast of it because the changes it introduces will generate the traditions for tomorrow's language learning.

During the 1980s, Zuboff (1988) studied how people's everyday lives were changing due to information technology. After nearly a decade, she had accumulated evidence to support the claim that information technology "not only produces action but also produces a voice that symbolically renders events, objects, and processes so that they become visible, knowable, and shareable in a new way" (p. 9). Zuboff coined the term **informating** to describe how desktop computers had not merely automated operations in the workplace but actually created a window through which to view processes.

informating:
Generating data about processes formerly invisible to the human eye.

The informating capacity of the Internet provides a glimpse into human language acquisition as it supports the sociopsychological processes learners engage in during online interactions and dialogue with others. Effective teaching–learning cycles in networked classrooms provide a way for teachers to become closer to their students' literacy development processes. The types of observations and instructional branching decisions teachers make during proximal instruction cannot be automated. In other words, the Internet cannot replace teachers and the roles they play in scaffolding students' literacy development. It can, however, help teachers visualize reading and writing processes in real time so they can respond appropriately to diversity in students' literacy development.

Where Do We Go From Here?

This book is meant to inspire teachers to view the Internet as a valuable component of the solution to the literacy crisis facing young adolescents, rather than as a resource to ban from literacy learning classrooms. The approach advocated in this book is for teachers to start with existing curriculum practices from nonnetworked classrooms to learn how Internet use can enhance those practices. From there, teachers can continue to increase their knowledge about how to maximize the full benefits or potential for literacy learning opportunities in networked classrooms. In order to do so adequately, teachers will need to connect professionally to other educators and parents and with community projects in the global village.

Truly understanding how literacy is affected by the Internet requires an interdisciplinary approach. The ongoing development of the Internet involves not only the citizens of the global village but also, on a deep infrastructure level, teams of professionals: computer scientists, artificial intelligence and natural language processing experts, knowledge engineers, technical communications workers, instructional designers, psychologists, and brain researchers. It is a challenge to keep up with new developments from their combined efforts. Internet innovations are fast paced and often unpredictable. As a result, teachers need to join online professional learning communities to stay abreast of technological developments affecting the nature of literacy and literacy learning.

Teachers who are ready for the challenge would be well served by collaborating with researchers from their local university to conduct action research, lesson studies, or design experiments to guide the design of interactive curricula and related classroom practices. The Internet transforms the teaching–learning cycle, and teachers need assistance with conducting rigorous inquiry about how it affects literacy achievement. Teachers who participate in online professional learning communities can engage in reflection and debate about the impacts technology has on their teaching practices and their students' learning (Shapiro & Levine, 1999). **Collaborative learning environments** are places where teachers can correspond during the planning phase and engage in reflection and evaluation about how well the design is supporting all students' literacy learning. Whatever type of evidence the focus of the evaluation calls for, teachers who engage in a study of inquiry about the effectiveness of their networked classroom practices will be equipped to confront the many unknowns that arise with technology in education (F.H. Wood & McQuarrie, 1999). Although the topic of how to evaluate technology in networked classrooms is beyond the scope of this book, it is an important aspect of designing innovative literacy opportunities for students.

Finally, the Internet may not replace printed materials or books in schools, but it can be an aid to teachers as they support and facilitate literacy development in the middle grades. The number of students reaching high school and even college with serious remedial reading problems in networked cultures is epidemic. Let us not make the mistake of assuming that if students have access to online resources, they will be able to engage successfully in independent reading, writing, and information research in networked classrooms. The networked classroom offers ample opportunity for teachers to intervene in students' literacy learning processes. Teachers must not assign their students a computer seat and then leave them to **surf** the Web without monitoring and learning about each student's unique literacy learning processes in order to make effective instructional decisions. In the networked classroom, teachers are not alone in their decision making. They can recruit trustworthy literacy mentors for themselves and their students from among those in the global village to help them bridge the digital literacy divide.

collaborative learning environment:
A password-protected workspace for groups.

surf:
To browse information on the Web leisurely.

GUIDING QUESTIONS FOR DISCUSSION

1. What are the new literacy challenges facing students in networked classrooms?

2. How do Internet accountability and policy changes affect literacy education?

3. How can teachers collaborate with other professionals to be better prepared to face the literacy challenges in networked classrooms?

This glossary contains a list of common technical terms related to Internet use. These terms also can serve as keywords when conducting online information research about topics related to information in this book. To use a glossary term in a search query, type the technical term into a search engine and combine it with a curriculum term of your own choosing.

asynchronous threaded discussion: An online forum for participants to communicate with each other in a time-delayed manner. Participants in the discussion do not need to be logged on at the same time.

blog: A Web log with dated entries that functions as an online journal that hosts opportunities for reader response interactions between the writer and audience.

blogosphere: The collective virtual community of blog writers, readers, and texts; term attributed to Brad Graham.

browser: An online interface used to access and read hypertext and interactive multimedia housed on the World Wide Web. Popular browsers include Internet Explorer and Netscape.

chat acronym: Slang used in online dialogue to save time with keystrokes; for example, *ASAP* means "as soon as possible"; *IMHO* means "in my humble/honest opinion"; *ty* means "thank you"; =^_^= means "same as above."

collaborative learning environment: A password-protected workspace for groups to conduct online communications and host information services designed to meet specific user needs; different Web applications provide various features.

computer network: A system of computers connected together by communication lines so that users can share information and common devices such as printers.

cybrary: An online library of World Wide Web resources compiled by educators working together to annotate website directories to share as special collections for specific curricular purposes.

digital authoring tools: Software applications that allow teachers and students to create hypertexts, interactive multimedia, or word-processed documents.

digital information literacy: Ability to locate online, evaluate, and apply digital information to build knowledge.

digital search: Strategic use of online search engines, indexes, and directories to locate resources applicable to an interactive curriculum in a particular content area.

domain: The Web address for an organizational or personal website.

emoticon: A group of keyboard characters used to express emotion in e-mail and other online communications. For example, ;-) represents a winking face.

e-notebook: A password-protected online student journal accessible to others in the collaborative learning environment.

Find command: A Web browser tool used to search on a page for a particular word.

flame war: A sequence of hostile messages exchanged online, usually in an Internet newsgroup or distributive learning community focused on a controversial topic.

global village: The combined membership of networked cultures around the world connected to each other via the Internet.

handheld remote: A portable device used to send wireless signals from a user to a computer or other receptor hardware; commonly part of a student response system.

hyperlink: Clickable text that connects to multimodal reading options within hypertext or interactive multimedia; term attributed to George Landow.

hypertext: Digital print that contains a multisequential text structure with hyperlinks readers click on to access other texts; term attributed to Ted Nelson.

hypertext link path: A reader's clickable text sequence when reading or surfing through hypertext or interactive multimedia.

informating: Generating data about processes formerly invisible to the human eye; a capacity of modern-day computers.

instant messaging: One-on-one online dialogue between two participants using the same communications software; commonly occurs in print format but also may occur through video or voice.

interactive multimedia: A system in which related blocks of multimodal information, such as digital video, photographs, sound, and text, are connected and can be presented together in a hyperlink structure. Also called *hypermedia*.

interactive whiteboard: A wall-mounted projection screen with touch sensors that control a computer connected to the Internet; used for group demonstrations and modeling or simulating Internet learning activities.

Internet: The hardware and programming infrastructure that connects information and communication network servers together globally, including communications networks such as e-mail and information networks such as the World Wide Web.

invisible Web: Online databases or subscription-only information not accessible to global search engines.

keyword search: A search engine query comprised of carefully selected words—such as professional vocabulary and related hyponyms, hypernyms, and synonyms—on a research topic.

lexia: A single block of narrative, images, sounds, or other media within a hypertext; multiple lexia are connected together through hyperlinks; from the Greek *lexis*, which means "to speak"; term attributed to George Landow.

log: An automated record of Internet activity.

local area network (LAN): Two or more computers connected by wires or a wireless networking application to a common server within a mile radius.

lurk: To read messages in a chat room or online forum without participating in the discussion.

multisequential: A characteristic of hypertext structures that allows for diverse reading options in a single hypertext.

netiquette: Online communication etiquette useful for managing group behavior and norms for discussion.

networked classroom: A physical environment in which students and teachers are connected to and use the Internet for educational purposes.

networked culture: A geographical community connected through Internet access to participants in the global village; members of networked cultures experience new modes of communication and information shared by others with whom they might not interact otherwise, such as people from different generations, social classes, and geographical locations.

online literacy learning: Reading, writing, and information research activities that occur via the Internet for instructional purposes.

online symposium: A gathering of invited guests for the purpose of showcasing student work and eliciting reader responses; can be hosted as a synchronous or asynchronous event using various forms of online dialogue and typically occurs in a collaborative learning environment.

open source: Software code and online applications produced by individuals for free download by anyone in the global community.

portable technology: Small technology devices that typically run on batteries and can be easily transported, for example, laptop computers, PDAs, cell phones.

post: A message submitted for the record during online dialogue among participants; for example, in a collaborative learning environment, students can post their opinions in an asynchronous threaded discussion that automatically displays the post or in a synchronous chat, which can be archived for later retrieval.

real time: Live interactions online such as in synchronous chats, as opposed to asynchronous e-mail or threaded discussions.

real-time authoring: The act of writing original texts for a live audience during synchronous communications such as chats or instant messaging.

search engine: An online program used to index the contents of registered websites and to provide search return lists in response to search queries, excluding the contents of the invisible Web; global search engines index portions of the World Wide Web and a site-specific search engine only indexes webpages within its host domain.

search query strategies: Purposeful combinations of keywords and operators used with a search engine to scan the Web for information on a specific topic of interest.

search return list: A collection of Web resources compiled by a search engine in response to a search query.

storyboard: A writing technique used to organize notes about characters and scenes into a story plot; may be produced in print or interactive multimedia formats.

student response system: A combination of software and hardware used to facilitate question-and-answer interactions between teachers and students via a wireless computer network and handheld remotes.

supportive text: Print enhanced with hyperlinks to text or interactive multimedia that elaborate, define, or explain content to scaffold students' comprehension at various reading levels; term attributed to Lynn Anderson-Inman and Mark Horney.

surf: To browse information on the Web leisurely.

synchronous chat: Real-time exchange of online dialogue between multiple participants logged on to the same Internet-based communications application at the same time; dialogue commonly occurs in print format but also may occur through video or voice.

thread: A running log of asynchronous posts on the same topic, for example, within an asynchronous discussion forum.

virtual communities: Groups whose members are connected through Internet access to each other for a specific purpose or through a common interest; members may include people from different generations, social classes, and geographical locations who may not otherwise interact.

wireless: Transmission of information or communications without cables or cords.

World Wide Web: Public portion of the Internet's online information resources; usually referred to as the Web.

REFERENCES

Aebersold, J.A., & Field, M.L. (1997). *From reader to reading teacher: Issues and strategies for second language classrooms.* Cambridge, England: Cambridge University Press.

Agre, P.E. (1999). Life after cyberspace. *EASST Review, 18*(3), 3–5.

Alexander, P.A. (2003). The development of expertise: The journey from acclimation to proficiency. *Educational Researcher, 32*(8), 10–14.

American Association of School Librarians & Association for Educational Communications and Technology. (1998). *Information power: Building partnerships for learning.* Chicago: American Library Association.

American Psychological Association (APA) Task Force on Psychology in Education. (1993, January). *Learner-centered psychological principles: Guidelines for school redesign and reform.* Washington, DC: American Psychological Association & Mid-Continent Regional Educational Laboratory.

American Psychological Association (APA) Work Group of the Board of Educational Affairs. (1997, November). *Learner-centered psychological principles: A framework for school reform and redesign.* Washington, DC: American Psychological Association.

Anderson-Inman, L., & Horney, M.A. (1998). Transforming text for at-risk readers. In D. Reinking, M.C. McKenna, L.D. Labbo, & R.D. Kieffer (Eds.), *Handbook of literacy and technology: Transformations in a post-typographic world* (pp. 15–44). Mahwah, NJ: Erlbaum.

Au, K.H. (1997, December). *Constructivist approaches, phonics, and the literacy learning of students of diverse backgrounds.* Presidential address at the National Reading Conference, Scottsdale, AZ.

Au, K.H., & Raphael, T.E. (2000). Equity and literacy in the next millennium. *Reading Research Quarterly, 35*(1), 170–188.

Baddeley, A., Logie, R., Nimmo-Smith, I., & Brereton, N. (1985). Components of fluent reading. *Journal of Memory and Language, 24*(1), 119–131.

Bandura, A. (1986). *Social foundations of thought and action: A social cognitive theory.* Englewood Cliffs, NJ: Prentice Hall.

Beach, R., & Lundell, D. (1998). Early adolescents' use of computer-mediated communication in writing and reading. In D. Reinking, M.C. McKenna, L.D. Labbo, & R.D. Kieffer (Eds.), *Handbook of literacy and technology: Transformations in a post-typographic world* (pp. 93–112). Mahwah, NJ: Erlbaum.

Becker, H.J. (1999). Internet use by teachers: Conditions of professional use and teacher-directed student use. *Teaching, learning, and computing: 1998 national survey* (Rep No.1). Irvine: Center for Research on Information Technology and Organizations, California University, Irvine; Duluth: University of Minnesota. Retrieved June 27, 2001, from http://www.crito.uci.edu/TLC/findings/internet-use/startpage.htm

Blachowicz, C.L.Z., & Fisher, P. (2000). Vocabulary instruction. In M.L. Kamil, P.B. Mosenthal, P.D. Pearson, & R. Barr (Eds.), *Handbook of reading research* (Vol. 3, pp. 503–523). Mahwah, NJ: Erlbaum.

Bolter, J.D. (1992). Literature in the electronic writing space. In M.C. Tuman (Ed.), *Literacy online: The promise (and peril) of reading and writing with computers* (pp. 19–42). Pittsburgh, PA: University of Pittsburgh Press.

Bolter, J.D. (1998). Hypertext and the question of visual literacy. In D. Reinking, M.C. McKenna, L.D. Labbo, & R.D. Kieffer (Eds.), *Handbook of literacy and technology: Transformations in a post-typographic world* (pp. 3–13). Mahwah, NJ: Erlbaum.

Boyer, E.L. (1995). *The basic school: A community for learning.* Princeton, NJ: Carnegie Foundation for the Advancement of Teaching.

Brandjes, E.C. (1997). *Teaching writing in a Web based classroom: A case study of Ted Nellen's "cyber English" class.* Retrieved February 17, 2003, from http://www.tnellen.com/cyber eng/lizcyber.html

Bransford, J.D. (2001). *Toward the development of a stronger community of educators: New opportunities made possible by integrating the learning sciences and technology* (Preparing Tomorrow's Teachers to Use Technology Vision Quest Technical Report). Lawrence, KS: Advanced Learning Technologies—Center for Research on Learning at the University of Kansas. Retrieved August 2, 2004, from http://www.pt3.org/VQ/html/bransford.html

Bransford, J.D., Brown, A.L., & Cocking, R.R. (Eds.). (1999). *How people learn: Brain, mind, experience, and school.* Washington, DC: National Academy Press.

Bransford, J.D., & Schwartz, D.L. (1999). Rethinking transfer: A simple proposal with multiple implications. In A. Iran-Nejad & P.D. Pearson (Eds.), *Review of research in education* (Vol. 24, pp. 61–100). Washington, DC: American Educational Research Association.

Burstein, J., Marcu, D., Andreyev, S., & Chodorow, M. (2001). Towards automatic classification of discourse elements in essays. *Proceedings of the 39th Annual Meeting of the Association for Computational Linguistics* (pp. 90–97). Toulouse, France: Association for Computational Linguistics.

Cassidy, J., & Cassidy, D. (December 2001/January 2002). What's hot, what's not for 2002. *Reading Today, 18*(3), pp. 1, 18–19.

Castleberg, L.W., & Closser, B. (2000). Minds across space: Teaching university writing consultants and high school writers to work together in the webbed writing center. *Kairos: A Journal for Teachers of Writing in Webbed Environments, 5*(1). Retrieved September 19, 2002, from http://english.ttu.edu/kairos/5.1/binder.html?coverweb/castlebergclosser/webconf.htm

Center for the Improvement of Early Reading Achievement (CIERA). (1998). *The CIERA survey of early literacy programs in high performing schools: Teacher survey.* Ann Arbor: CIERA, University of Michigan.

Chung, G.K.W.K., & O'Neil, H.F., Jr. (1997). *Methodological approaches to online scoring of essays* (Center for the Study of Evaluation Technical Report No. 461). Retrieved June 24, 2004, from University of California, Los Angeles, National Center for Research on Evaluation, Standards, and Student Testing website: http://www.cse.ucla.edu/CRESST/Reports/TECH461.PDF

Cognition and Technology Group at Vanderbilt. (1997). *The Jasper Project: Lessons in curriculum, instruction, assessment, and professional development.* Mahwah, NJ: Erlbaum.

Collier, C. (2004). *Seeking meaning: A process approach to library and information services* (2nd ed.). Westport, CT: Libraries Unlimited.

D'Agostino, K.N., & Varone, S.D. (1991). Interacting with basic writers in the computer classroom. *Computers and Composition, 8*(3), 39–49.

Dewey, J. (1990). *The school and society and the child and the curriculum.* Chicago: The University of Chicago Press.

Donahue, P., Voelkl, K., Campbell, J., & Mazzeo, J. (March 1999). *NAEP 1998 Reading Report Card for the nation and the states.* Washington, DC: U.S. Department of Education, Office of Educational Research and Improvement.

Donin, J., Bracewell, R.J., Frederiksen, C.H., & Dillinger, M. (1992). Students' strategies for writing instructions organizing conceptual information in text. *Written Communication, 9*(2), 209–236.

Eisenberg, M.B., & Berkowitz, R.E. (2000). *Teaching information and technology skills: The Big 6 in secondary schools.* Worthington, OH: Linworth. (ERIC Document Reproduction Service No. ED449780)

English-Lueck, J.A. (1998, June). *Technology and social change: The effects on family and community.* Paper presented at the Consortium of Social Sciences (COSSA) Congressional Seminar. Retrieved February 12, 2003, from http://www.sjsu.edu/depts/anthropology/svcp/SVCPcosa.html

Feuerstein, R., Klein, P.S., & Tannenbaum, A.J. (Eds.). (1991). *Mediated learning experience (MLE): Theoretical, psychosocial, and learning implications.* London: Freund.

Finders, M.J. (1997). *Just girls: Hidden literacies and life in junior high.* New York: Teachers College Press.

Flower, L., & Hayes, J.R. (1980). The dynamics of composing: Making plans and juggling constraints. In L.W. Gregg & E.R. Steinberg (Eds.), *Cognitive processes in writing* (pp. 31–50). Hillsdale, NJ: Erlbaum.

Foltz, P.W., Gilliam, S., & Kendall, S. (2000). Supporting content-based feedback in online writing evaluation with LSA. *Interactive Learning Environments, 8*(2), 111–129.

Friedman, T.L. (2005). *The world is flat: A brief history of the twenty-first century.* New York: Farrar Straus Giroux.

Fukuda-Parr, S., & Birdsall, N. (2001). *Human development report 2001: Making new technologies work for human development.* New York: Oxford University Press for the United Nations Development Programme. Retrieved February 10, 2002, from http://www.undp.org/hdr2001

Gardner, H. (1993). *Multiple intelligences: The theory in practice.* New York: Basic Books.

Garner, R., & Gillingham, M.G. (1998). The Internet in the classroom: Is it the end of transmission-oriented pedagogy? In D. Reinking, M.C. McKenna, L.D. Labbo, & R.D. Kieffer (Eds.), *Handbook of literacy and technology: Transformations in a post-typographic world* (pp. 221–231). Mahwah, NJ: Erlbaum.

Gates, B. (2005, February 15). Keynote address. National Education Summit on High Schools, Washington, DC.

George, P.S., & Lounsbury, J.H. (2000). *Making big schools feel small: Multiage grouping, looping, and schools-within-a-school.* Westerville, OH: National Middle School Association.

Guillaume, A.M. (2000). *Classroom teaching: A primer for new professionals.* Upper Saddle River, NJ: Prentice Hall.

Hadlow, M. (2002). Kabul University goes on-line. Retrieved October 12, 2003, from http://www.unesco.org/webworld/news/2002/021011_afghanistan.shtml

Haney, J.J., Lumpe, A.T., Czerniak, C.M., & Egan, V. (2002). From beliefs to actions: The beliefs and actions of teachers implementing change. *Journal of Science Teacher Education, 13*(3), 171–187.

Harris, T.L., & Hodges, R.E. (Eds.). (1995). *The literacy dictionary: The vocabulary of reading and writing.* Newark, DE: International Reading Association.

Heller, R.S. (1990). The role of hypermedia in education: A look at the research issues. *Journal of Research on Computing in Education, 22*(4), 431–441.

Hermans, B. (1997). Intelligent software agents on the Internet. *First Monday, 2*(3). Retrieved August 26, 2005, from http://www.firstmonday.dk/issues/issue2_3/ch_123

Hermans, B. (1998). Desperately seeking help: Helping hands and human touch. *First Monday, 3*(11). Retrieved August 26, 2005, from http://www.firstmonday.dk/issues/issue3_11/hermans

International Reading Association (IRA). (2002). *What is evidence-based reading instruction?* (Position statement). Newark, DE: Author.

International Reading Association (IRA) & National Association for the Education of Young Children. (1998). *Learning to read and write: Developmentally appropriate practices for young children* (Position statement). Newark, DE, & Washington, DC: Authors.

International Reading Association (IRA) & National Council of Teachers of English. (1996). *Standards for the English language arts*. Newark, DE, & Urbana, IL: Authors.

International Society for Technology in Education (ISTE). (1999). *National educational technology standards for students*. Eugene, OR: Author. Retrieved August 30, 2005, from http://cnets.iste.org

International Society for Technology in Education (ISTE). (2002). *National educational technology standards for teachers: Preparing teachers to use technology*. Eugene, OR: Author. Retrieved August 30, 2005, from http://cnets.iste.org

Johnson, M.J. (2001, April 4). *The effectiveness of the Children's Internet Protection Act (CHIPA)*. Washington, DC: Congressional Subcommittee on Telecommunications and the Internet. Retrieved February 3, 2003, from http://energycommerce.house.gov/107/hearings/04042001Hearing155/print.htm

Joram, E., Woodruff, E., Bryson, M., & Lindsay, P.H. (1992). The effects of revising with a word processor on written composition. *Research in the Teaching of English, 26*(2), 167–192.

Judge, P. (2000, March 2). A lesson in computer literacy from India's poorest kids. *BusinessWeek Online*. Retrieved October 20, 2002, from http://www.businessweek.com/bwdaily/dnflash/mar2000/nf00302b.htm

Just, M.A., & Carpenter, P.A. (1992). A capacity theory of comprehension: Individual differences in working memory. *Psychological Review, 99*(1), 122–149.

Kamil, M.L. (2003). *Adolescents and literacy: Reading for the 21st century*. Washington, DC: Alliance for Excellent Education.

Kamil, M.L., Intrator, S.M., & Kim, H.S. (2000). The effects of other technologies on literacy and literacy learning. In M.L. Kamil, P.B. Mosenthal, P.D. Pearson, & R. Barr (Eds.), *Handbook of reading research* (Vol. 3, pp. 771–788). Mahwah, NJ: Erlbaum.

Kintsch, E., Steinhart, D., Stahl, G., & LSA Research Group. (2000). Developing summarization skills through the use of LSA-based feedback. *Interactive Learning Environments, 8*(2), 87–109.

Konishi, M. (2003). Strategies for reading hypertext by Japanese ELS learners. *The Reading Matrix, 3*(3). Retrieved August 30, 2005, from http://www.readingmatrix.com/articles/konishi/article.pdf

Kozma, R.B. (Ed.). (2003). *Technology, innovation, and educational change: A global perspective*. Eugene, OR: International Society for Technology in Education.

Kraut, R., Patterson, M., Lundmark, V., Kiesler, S., Mukopadhyay, T., & Scherlis, W. (1998). Internet paradox: A social technology that reduces social involvement and psychological well-being? *American Psychologist, 53*(9), 1017–1031.

Lance, K.C., & Loertscher, D.V. (2005). *Powering achievement: School library media programs make a difference: The evidence* (3rd ed.). San Jose, CA: Hi Willow Research and Publishing.

Landow, G.P. (1992). *Hypertext: The convergence of contemporary critical theory and technology*. Baltimore: Johns Hopkins University Press.

Leu, D.J., Jr. (2000). Our children's future: Changing the focus of literacy and literacy instruction. *The Reading Teacher, 53*(5), 424–429.

Leu, D.J., Jr. (2001). Internet project: Preparing students for new literacies in a global village. *The Reading Teacher, 54*(6), 568–572.

Leu, D.J., Jr., & Kinzer, C.K. (2000). The convergence of literacy instruction with networked technologies for information and communication. *Reading Research Quarterly, 35*(1), 108–127.

Levine, M. (2002). *Educational care: A system for understanding and helping children with learning differences at home and in school* (2nd ed.). Cambridge, MA: Educators Publishing Service.

Lockard, J., & Abrams, P.D. (2004). *Computers for 21st century educators* (6th ed.). Boston: Allyn & Bacon.

McAninch, A.R. (1993). *Teacher thinking and the case method: Theory and future directions.* New York: Teachers College Press.

McKenna, M.C. (1998). Electronic texts and the transformation of beginning reading. In D. Reinking, M.C. McKenna, L.D. Labbo, & R.D. Kieffer (Eds.), *Handbook of literacy and technology: Transformations in a post-typographic world* (pp. 45–59). Mahwah, NJ: Erlbaum.

McNabb, M.L. (1996). *Toward a theory of proximal instruction: Pedagogical practices for composition within a computerized learning environment.* Unpublished doctoral dissertation, Northern Illinois University, DeKalb.

McNabb, M.L. (2001, June). *Emerging assessment principles.* Paper presented at the National Educational Computing Conference, Chicago.

McNabb, M.L. (2004, April). *Closing the achievement gap with technology-supported classroom assessments.* Paper presented at the American Educational Research Association Annual Meeting, San Diego, CA.

McNabb, M.L., Hassel, B., & Steiner, L. (2002). Literacy learning on the net: An exploratory study. *Reading Online, 5*(10). Retrieved September 14, 2004, from http://www.reading online.org/articles/art_index.asp?HREF=/articles/mcnabb/index.html

McNabb, M.L., & Smith, S.C. (1998). Proximal instruction strategies and assessment tools for managing performance-based learning. In *20th Annual Selected Research Proceedings of the 1997 National Conference of the Association for Educational Technology and Communication* (pp. 261–279). St. Louis, MO: Association for Educational Technology and Communication.

Miller, P.H. (1993). *Theories of developmental psychology* (3rd ed.). New York: Freeman.

Moore, D.W., Bean, T.W., Birdyshaw, D., & Rycik, J.A. (1999). *Adolescent literacy: A position statement for the Commission on Adolescent Literacy of the International Reading Association.* Newark, DE: International Reading Association.

Murnane, R.J., & Levy, F. (1996). *Teaching the new basic skills: Principles for educating children to thrive in a changing economy.* New York: Free Press.

National Institute of Child Health and Human Development (NICHD). (2000). *Report of the National Reading Panel. Teaching children to read: An evidence-based assessment of the scientific research literature on reading and its implications for reading instruction* (NIH Publication No. 00-4769). Washington, DC: U.S. Government Printing Office.

National Middle School Association (NMSA). (2003a). *Research and resources in support of This We Believe.* Columbus, OH: Author.

National Middle School Association (NMSA). (2003b). *This we believe: Successful schools for young adolescents.* Columbus, OH: Author.

Nie, N.H., & Erbing, L. (2000). *Internet and society: A preliminary report.* Stanford, CA: Stanford Institute for the Quantitative Study of Society.

Nielsen, J. (2005, January 31). *Usability of websites for teenagers.* Retrieved February 15, 2005, from http://www.useit.com/alertbox/20050131.html

No Child Left Behind Act of 2001 (NCLB), Pub. L. No. 107-110, 115 Stat. 1425 (2002).

Norris, C., & Soloway, E. (2000, September). *The Snapshot Survey Service: A website for assessing teachers' and administrators' technology activities, beliefs, and needs.* Paper presented at the Secretary's Conference on Educational Technology, Alexandria, VA. Retrieved October 10, 2005, from http://www.ed.gov/rschstat/eval/tech/techconfoo/cathienorris.pdf

O'Neill, E.T., Lavoie, B.F., & Bennett, R. (2003). Trends in the evolution of the public Web. *D-Lib Magazine, 9*(4). Retrieved November 20, 2004, from http://dlib.org/dlib/april03/lavoie/04lavoie.html

Paul, T.D. (1996). *Patterns of reading practice.* Madison, WI: Institute for Academic Excellence.

Pellegrino, J.W., Chudowsky, N., & Glaser, R. (Eds.). (2001). *Knowing what students know: The science and design of educational assessment.* Washington, DC: National Academy Press. Retrieved May 24, 2002, from http://www.nap.edu/books/0309072727/html

Purcell-Gates, V. (1997). Focus on research: The future of research in language arts. *Language Arts, 74*(2), 280–283.

Rasinski, T.V., Padak, N.D., McKeon, C.A., Wilfong, L.G., Friedauer, J.A., & Heim, P. (2005). Is reading fluency a key for successful high school reading? *Journal of Adolescent & Adult Literacy, 49*(1), 22–27.

Reinking, D., & Bridwell-Bowles, L. (1996). Computers in reading and writing. In M.L. Kamil, P.B. Mosenthal, P.D. Pearson, & R. Barr (Eds.), *Handbook of reading research* (Vol. 3, pp. 310–340). Mahwah, NJ: Erlbaum.

Riel, M. (2000). New designs for connected teaching and learning. *Proceedings of the Secretary's Conference on Educational Technology—2000.* Retrieved September 10, 2000, from http://www.gse.uci.edu/mriel/whitepaper/learning.html

Riel, M., & Harasim, L. (1994). Research perspectives on network learning. *Machine-Mediated Learning, 4*(2 & 3), 91–113.

Romiszowski, A. (1997). The use of telecommunication in education. In S. Dijkstra, N.M. Seel, F. Schott, & R.D. Tennyson (Eds.), *Instructional design: International perspectives: Solving instructional design problems* (pp. 183–220). Mahwah, NJ: Erlbaum.

Rose, D.H., & Meyer, A., with Strangman, N., & Rappolt, G. (2002). *Teaching every student in the digital age: Universal design for learning.* Alexandria, VA: Association for Supervision and Curriculum Development.

Rouet, J.F., Levonen, J.J., Dillon, A., & Spiro, R.J. (Eds.). (1996). *Hypertext and cognition.* Mahwah, NJ: Erlbaum.

Scardamalia, M., & Bereiter, C. (1986). Research on written composition. In M.C. Wittrock (Ed.), *Handbook of research on teaching* (3rd ed., pp. 778–803). New York: Macmillan.

Schunk, D.H. (1991). *Learning theories: An educational perspective.* New York: Macmillan.

Sen, A., Partelow, L., & Miller, D.C. (2005). *Comparative indicators of education in the United States and other G8 countries: 2004* (NCES 2005-021). U.S. Department of Education, National Center for Education Statistics. Washington, DC: U.S. Government Printing Office.

Serim, F., & Salpeter, J. (2003). *Making the grade: Accountability and assessment under No Child Left Behind* [Technical report/monograph]. Washington, DC: Consortium of School Networking.

Shapiro, N.S., & Levine, J.H. (1999). *Creating learning communities: A practical guide to winning support, organizing for change, and implementing programs.* San Francisco: Jossey-Bass.

Shea, V. (2004a). Introduction. *The core rules of netiquette*. Retrieved February 17, 2004, from http://www.albion.com/netiquette/introduction.html

Shea, V. (2004b). Rule 3: Know where you are in cyberspace. *The core rules of netiquette*. Retrieved February 17, 2004, from http://www.albion.com/netiquette/rule3.html

Shields, M.K., & Behrman, R.E. (2000). Children and computer technology: Analysis and recommendations. *The future of children: Children and computer technology*, *10*(2), 4–30. Retrieved January 16, 2000, from http://www.futureofchildren.org/usr_doc/vol10no2Art1.pdf

Tapscott, D. (1998). *Growing up digital: The rise of the net generation*. New York: McGraw-Hill.

Vygotsky, L.S. (1978). *Mind in society: The development of higher psychological processes* (M. Cole, V. John-Steiner, S. Scribner, & E. Souberman, Eds. & Trans.). Cambridge, MA: Harvard University Press. (Original work published 1934)

Wallace, P. (1999). *The psychology of the Internet*. Cambridge, England: Cambridge University Press.

Walz, J. (2001). Reading hypertext: Lower-level processes. *Canadian Modern Language Review*, *57*(3), 475–494.

Wenger, M.J., & Payne, D.G. (1996). Human information processing correlates of reading hypertext. *Technical Communication*, *43*(1), 51–60.

Wiggins, G.P. (1993). *Assessing student performance: Exploring the purpose and limits of testing*. San Francisco: Jossey-Bass.

Williams, B.T. (2004). "A puzzle to the rest of us": Who is a "reader" anyway? *Journal of Adolescent & Adult Literacy*, *47*(8), 686–689.

Williams, W., & Sternberg, R.J. (1988). Group intelligence: Why some groups are better than others. *Intelligence*, *12*(4), 351–377.

Wood, F.H., & McQuarrie, F. (1999). On-the-job learning. *Journal of Staff Development*, *20*(30), 10–13.

Wood, J.M. (2000). *A marriage waiting to happen: Computers and process writing*. New York: Education Development Center. Retrieved November 17, 2002, from http://www.edtech leaders.org/resources/readings/upperelemliteracy/wood_computerswriting.htm

Zuboff, S. (1988). *In the age of the smart machine: The future of work and power*. New York: Basic Books.

Literature Cited

Rowling, J.K. (2003). *Harry Potter and the Order of the Phoenix*. New York: Scholastic.

Twain, M. (2003). *The adventures of Huckleberry Finn*. New York: Penguin Putnam. (Original work published 1884)

INDEX

Note: Page numbers followed by *f* and *t* indicate figures and tables, respectively.

HUCK FINN'S JOURNEY INTERDISCIPLINARY UNIT:
activities in, 41*t*; assessment in, 43–44,
53–55; asynchronous threaded
discussions in, 42, 47; critical reading
in, 43, 48; cybrary for, 39–40; daily
tasks of, 40–41; feedback in, 43, 44;
learning environment for, 42–43;
learning opportunities in, 38*f*;
literature circles in, 42–52; netiquette
in, 42; online dialogues in, 46–52;
online research in, 39–40; overview of,
37–39; proximal instruction in, 44–52;
reading comprehension in, 43–52;
route maps, 44–45, 51–55; spelling
errors in, 42–43; Web resources for, 40*t*
HUMAN BODY SYSTEMS. *See* Understanding
Human Body Systems unit
HUMAN LANGUAGE: Internet's effect on,
126–128; versus programming
language, 57
HYPERLINKS, 21, 58
HYPERTEXT, viii; comprehension strategies
for reading, 22; and online research
demands, 23–25; reading skills
required for, 20–23; structure of, 21; as
teaching aid, 116
HYPERTEXT LINK PATHS, 118

I

ICEBREAKER ACTIVITIES, 31
IDENTITY DEVELOPMENT, 5, 29, 80
ILLINOIS MATHEMATICS AND SCIENCE ACADEMY,
70
INDEPENDENT READING, 13
INDIA, 124–125. *See also* Mitra, S.
INDIVIDUALIZED INSTRUCTION, 14–15
INDUSTRIAL COUNTRIES, 123
INFORMATING, 128
INFORMATION DELIVERY, 2–3
INFORMATION LITERACY STANDARDS FOR
STUDENT LEARNING, 63
INFORMATION SEARCH. *See* research, online
INFORMATIONAL TEXTS, 20, 123
INSTANT MESSAGING, 79, 119
INSTRUCTIONAL PRACTICES: common
difficulties involving, 14; data-driven
decisions for, 16; importance of, 8;
online literacy learning benefits to, ix;

recommendations for, 14. *See also*
specific practices
INTERACTIVE CURRICULUM: design of, 11, 103,
105–108; in Harry Potter Online
Writers' Workshop, 84*f*, 85–87; in Huck
Finn's Journey unit, 38*f*, 39–41; and
organizing networked classrooms, 7*f*;
supportive texts in, 23; in
Understanding Human Body Systems
unit, 62*f*, 63–66
INTERACTIVE MULTIMEDIA, viii; definition of,
60; for minilessons, 71; process of, 70;
studies of, 60
INTERACTIVE WHITEBOARD, 63, 70
INTERNATIONAL READING ASSOCIATION (IRA),
5, 15, 105
INTERNATIONAL SOCIETY FOR TECHNOLOGY IN
EDUCATION (ISTE), x–xi, xiv, 63, 85, 106
INTERNET: policies affecting use of, 6–7, 35
INTERNET PUBLIC LIBRARY, 107*t*
INTRATOR, S.M., 9, 20, 60
INVISIBLE WEB, 58
IRA. *See* International Reading
Association (IRA)
IRONY, 50
ISTE. *See* International Society for
Technology in Education (ISTE)

J

JOHNSON, M.J., 64
JORAM, E., 26
JUDGE, P., 1, 59
JUST, M.A., 21

K

KABUL UNIVERSITY, 3
KAMIL, M.L., 9, 20, 36, 60, 122
KENDALL, S., 114
KEYBOARDING, 55
KEYWORDS, 71–73
KIESLER, S., 33
KIM, H.S., 9, 20, 60
KINTSCH, E., 114
KINZER, C.K., 4, 9, 15, 20, 80
KLEIN, P.S., 29
KNOWLEDGE-CENTERED CLASSROOMS, 10–11.
See also interactive curriculum

N

NAEP. *See* National Assessment of Educational Progress (NAEP)

NARRATIVES: assessment for writing, 89–92; drafting process in, 97–98; prewriting for, 92–96; questions for writing, 89*t*; revision of, 98–99; students' choice of, 123; study of, 85; text structure of, 20

NATIONAL ASSESSMENT OF EDUCATIONAL PROGRESS (NAEP), 13

NATIONAL ASSOCIATION FOR THE EDUCATION OF YOUNG CHILDREN, 5

NATIONAL COUNCIL OF TEACHERS OF ENGLISH, 105

NATIONAL EDUCATIONAL TECHNOLOGY STANDARDS FOR STUDENTS (NETS-S), x, 63, 85, 106

NATIONAL EDUCATIONAL TECHNOLOGY STANDARDS FOR TEACHERS (NETS-T), xi

NATIONAL INSTITUTE OF CHILD HEALTH AND HUMAN DEVELOPMENT, 13, 37

NATIONAL MIDDLE SCHOOL ASSOCIATION (NMSA), 5, 14, 18, 27, 29, 32, 80, 111

NATIONAL READING INITIATIVE, 124

NELSON, T., 20

NETIQUETTE: definition of, 29; establishing rules for, 109–110; in Harry Potter Online Writers' Workshop, 88–89; in Huck Finn's Journey unit, 42; for online writing circles, 88–89; rationale for, 30

NETS-S. *See National Educational Technology Standards for Students* (NETS-S)

NETS-T. *See National Educational Technology Standards for Teachers* (NETS-T)

NETWORKED CLASSROOM DESIGN: first step in, 103–108; fourth step in, 103, 116–120; second step in, 103, 108–112; third step in, 103, 112–116

NETWORKED CLASSROOMS: characteristics of, 8–11; definition of, xi; importance of scaffolding in, 14; introduction of, 102; model for, 7–8; organization of, 7*f*

NETWORKED CULTURE, vii, 25. *See also* learning problems

NIE, N.H., 1

NIELSEN, J., 35–36

NIMMO-SMITH, I., 21

NMSA. *See* National Middle School Association (NMSA)

NO CHILD LEFT BEHIND ACT OF 2001, x, 124

NONINVASIVE TEACHING TECHNIQUES, 2

NONVERBAL CUES, 31

NORRIS, C., viii

NORTHWEST REGIONAL EDUCATIONAL LABORATORY, 83*t*

NORTHWESTERN UNIVERSITY, 85

NOTE-TAKING, 118–119

O

OBJECTIVES, 105–107

OBSERVATIONS, 117

O'NEIL, H.F., JR., 114

O'NEILL, E.T., 58

ONLINE CHATS, 28. *See also specific types*

ONLINE DIALOGUES: characteristics of, 79; cognitive demands of, 27–28; in Huck Finn's Journey unit, 46–52; trust required for, 31

ONLINE LITERACY LEARNING: benefits of, ix; definition of, vii; versus print-based literacy learning, viii; rationale for, 5–6

ONLINE RESEARCH. *See* research, online

ONLINE SYMPOSIUM, 87, 99

ONLINE WRITING AND COMMUNICATION CENTER, 83*t*

ONLINE WRITING CIRCLES: assessment of, 89–92; behavior in, 88–89; benefits of, 83; drafting process in, 97–98; in Harry Potter Online Writers' Workshop, 88–89; prewriting in, 92–96; proximal instruction in, 92–99; publishing stage of, 99–100; revision in, 98–99

OPEN SOURCE CODE, 107

OPERATORS, 71

OWNERSHIP, OF LITERACY, 36–38, 123, 125; related to autonomy, 14. *See also* learner-centered classrooms, self-regulation

P

PADAK, N.D., 123–124

PARENT INVOLVEMENT, 87, 89

PARTELOW, L., 36

PARTICIPATION, 30

PASSWORD-PROTECTED WEBSITES, 64

PATTERSON, M., 33

PAUL, T.D., 13, 123